VITTORIO SERRA

New practic

Churches

Museums

Monuments

Fountains

The recently restored Last Supper

Useful information

Via dei Rustici 5 - 50122 Florence, Italy
Tel. (+39) 055 239.82.24
Fax (+39) 055 21 63 66
E-mail: bbonechi@dada.it
E-mail: barbara@bonechionline.com
http//www.bonechionline.com
Printed in Italy

Managing Editor: Barbara Bonechi
Graphics: Nunzia Trabucco
Layout : Media Studio - Florence
Associate Editor and Picture Researcher: Lorena Lazzari
Revision and up-dating: Giuliano Valdes, Editing studio - Pisa
Useful information collected by: Giuliano Valdes
Photographic credits: Bonechi Ed. "Il Turismo" S.r.l; Fabio Stella;
Archivio Scrocchi, Milan.
Aerial photographs: property of Bonechi, taken by Pubbli Aer Foto; page 49
- Aut S.M.A. 327/74; page 93, top - Aut. S.M.A. 401/69; page 118 - Aut, S.M.A.
401/69 and I-Buga, Milan; page 9, bottom - Aut. S.M.A. 256/82
Last Supper (Church of Santa Maria delle Grazie) by kind concession of the
Ministero per i Beni e le Attività Culturali - Milan.
Photo-lithographs: Cartografica Ciulli, Florence
Printed by: BO.BA.DO.MA, Florence
ISBN 88-7204-438-3

*This guide book states where the various works of art were located at the time of printing

Evangelist; King Solomon; The Sybil Samia) and G. B. Moroni (*Portrait of Michel de l'Hopital*).

Room XIII - This room is named after Nicolò da Bologna and is dedicated to works by Italian and Flemish artists of the end of the 16th century and the 17th century, including Fede Galizia (*Portrait of Paolo Morigia*), Isaac Soreau (*Still Life*), Jan Van Kessel (*Birds in a Swamp*), Henrick or Barent Avercamp (*Winter Landscape*), and Guido Reni (*Mary Magdalene Penitent*).

Room XIV - Works by 17th century Italian painters, including Orazio Borgianni (*The Three Hundred Christian Martyrs*) and Evaristo Baschenis (*Still-life with Musical Instruments*).

Room XV - Paintings by 17th century Lombard artists, including Giuseppe Vermiglio (*Judith and Holfernes; Jael and Sisera*) G. Cesare Procaccini (*St. Michael Archangel), Morazzone (*Adoration of the Magi*)) Daniele Crespi (*S. Filippo Benizzi).*

Room XVI - More paintings by Lombard painters of the 17th century including: *Death of Cleopatra* by Francesco Cairo; *Female Allegorical Figure* by Giovanni Serodino; *Mary Magdalene; Susanna and the Elders; Holy Family* by C. Francesco Nuvolone, *Mary Magdalene* by G. Cesare Procaccini, *Portrait of Manfredo Settala* by Daniele Crespi.

Room XVII - Italian artists of the end of the 17th century and the 18th century. Of particular interest are: Giandomenico Tiepolo (*Bust of a Bishop; Presentation of Christ at the Temple),* G. Francesco Castiglione (*Rebecca at the Fountain*), Fra' Galgario (*Portrait of a Young Man*), Cesare Ligari (*Moses and the Serpent of Bronze),* A. Raphael Mengs (*Portrait of Leopold II of Hapsburg Lorraine).*

Room XVIII - The De Pecis Collection is displayed in this room. Among the most noteworthy paintings are: *The Elderly Spinner among Poultry* by the VH Monogram Painter, several fine paintings by Giambattista Gigola (*Bradamant in Merlin's Cave; Bernabò Visconti at the Castle of Trezzo; Giovanni Edoardo and Maria de Pecis; Ludovico il Moro at the Tomb of Beatrice d'Este; Boccaccio's Brigade*), and works by Gaspare Landi (*Girl with a Funerary Urn*) Andrea Appiani (*Portrait of Carolina Pitrot Angiolini*); also, examples of Milanese art of various eras: *Monument to Andrea Appiani, The Entrance of Emperor Francis I into Milan,*

Ambrosian Picture Gallery, Basket of Fruit by Caravaggio

Horses, Hebe, Table with Fish in the Center. Also displayed in this room are Antonio Canova's *Self-portrait* and Bertel Thorvaldsen's *Self-portrait.*

Room XIX - Italian paintings of the end of the 19th and the beginning of the 20th century. The most noteworthy are: Andrea Appiani (*Female Portrait, Portrait of Napoleon Bonaparte*), Francesco Hayez (*Portraits, Mary Magdalene*), Giovanni Migliara (*The Charterhouse of Pavia, The Arch of Peace in Milan*), Domenico Induno (*Girl at the Fountain, Old Man with a Dog*), Girolamo Induno (*Porta S. Pancrazio in Rome, Visit to the Field*) Massimo *D'Azeglio (Alpine Scene, Landscape*), Mosè Bianchi (*Motherhood, Riding Horseback, Nuns at the Shore, The Shepherd's House, Sheep at the Stream, Boating, Paolo and Francesca, Flora*), Emilio Longoni (*Shut out of School*).

Room XX - The Peristyle or colonnade connects the Library to the old Room of the Doctors; it can be visited upon request.

Room XXI - This room contains Flemish and German paintings of the 14th to the 16th centuries. Particularly worthy of note are works by: Master of the Tucher Altar (*Madonna and Child*), Master of the Female Half-Figures (*Mary Magdalene*), Andries Daneels (*Madonna and Child in a Garland of Flowers*), Jan Brueghel the Younger (*The Original Sin, Expulsion from Paradise*), Giuseppe Bertini (*Vetrata Dantesca*), Cornelis Van Cleve (*Madonna and Child with St. John*), Geertgen tot Sint Jans (*Madonna and Child*).

Room XXII - Frescoes and sculpture are displayed in this room, including examples of Roman art of the 2nd to the 4th century A.D. (*fragment of a sarcophagus, head of a man, head of a child*), works by G. Antonio Piatti (*Plato*) and Bambaia (*Reliefs from the Tomb of Gaston de Foix, Jesus Faces Caiaphas, Ecce Homo, The Ascent to Calvary, Jesus Denuded*). Of special interest also are the frescoes of *Saints* by a Lombard painter of the end of the 14th - beginning of the 15th century.

Room XXIII - This room is temporarily being used as a picture gallery, but will eventually contain the scientific collections from the Settala Museum.

Room XXIV - This room is called the Luini room and can be visited only upon request. A fresco by Bernardo Luini, *The Incoronation of the Virgin* is displayed here.

From the atrium it is possible to gain access to the **Ambrosian Library**. This is the prestigious institution which was founded and opened to the public in 1609 by Cardinal Federico Borromeo, archbishop of Milan. The Cardinal endowed the library with manuscript codices and books from countries throughout Europe and Asia. It has grown over the centuries and now has 35.000 manuscripts, 3.000 incunabula and 750.000 books and periodicals. Among the most famous manuscripts we note *Ilias Picta*, a Greco-Byzantine manuscript of the 5th - 6th century, illuminated with Classical illustrations; the 14th century *Virgil* with illuminations by Simone Martini which belonged to Petrarch and has his handwritten notes; the palimpsests of Cicero and Plato; the 1353 *Divine Comedy;* the *Irish Codex*; the *Provenzal Codex*, the *Gothic Ulfilas* and the famous *Atlantic Codex* (hand-written by Leonardo da Vinci himself). There are numerous *Papyri, Books of Hours*, parchments and illuminated codices and also great Master drawings.

Fifth Itinerary

1 Church of Sant'Eustorgio
2 Basilica of San Lorenzo Maggiore
3 Church of Santa Maria della Passione
4 Church of Santa Maria at San Satiro
5 Church of Santa Maria at San Celso
6 Church of San Carlo al Corso
7 The Lazzaretto
8 Church of San Nazaro Maggiore
9 Church of San Simpliciano
10 The Naviglio Canal
11 The Main Hospital

Church of Sant'Eustorgio

St. Eustorgius is one of the most remarkable Medieval monuments in Milan. We do not know when the church was first started and only a few stones of the tiny basilica, which was built in the 4th century over the burial place of archbishop St. Eustorgius, are left. It was incorporated into the structure of the larger church constructed on the site towards the end of the 11th century in Romanesque-Cluniac style. The church was almost totally destroyed by the Emperor Frederick I Barbarossa who, in 1164 removed the relics which were believed to be of the Three Kings (the Magi) and which, according to tradition, were given to St. Eustorgius by Emperor Constantine, and had them taken to Cologne. In the 13th century the reconstruction in Romanesque style was begun and the beautiful apse, with its external arches on the upper register, is from this period. The most important transformations took place in 1220 when the Dominicans moved in and then, after the death of St. Peter Martyr in 1252, a complete remodeling of the church commenced and went on for several centuries. The right side is totally occupied by a series of private family chapels protruding into the main

Church of Sant'Eustorgio, aerial view

Church of Sant'Eustorgio, side view

body of the church: first come the 15th century ones, then the 14th century ones with arches at the lower level and ogival or monoforus or biforus mullioned windows. The 13th century transept chapels also protrude from the main church structure in a similar manner. Next to the Romanesque apse we find the pointed bell-tower, which is 243 feet tall and was built in the years 1279-1309. It is a typical Lombard campanile with mullioned openings in the bell-chamber. Next, after a 15th century chapel, comes the graceful exterior of the famous *Portinari Chapel* of the same period, with its square body and polygonal drum. The façade of the church (renovated in 1863-65) has three portals and five windows; the two side ones and the central window are biforus. The decorated frieze along the top of the façade and the little brick arches are part of the original façade. On the left corner, is a stone edicola supported on one side by a column, built in 1597 to replace the original wooden one from which, according to local tradition, St. Peter Martyr preached.

Interior -It is 227 feet long and 78 feet wide, it has three naves divided into eight spans by large pillars with typical 11th to13th century type capitals carved with little monstrous figures and entwined branches. The fourth pillar to the left is interesting: it shows the *Urn of the Magi being carried in procession.*

Church of Sant'Eustorgio, stone edicola on the façade

In the right aisle after the third chapel, the spans are incorporated into the chapels that follow. The first chapel, of the *Brivio Family*, was constructed in 1484 and restored in the 19th century. The triptych with *Madonna and Saints* is by Bergognone. On the left wall, the *Funeral Monument to Giovanni Stefano Brivio* (died 1484) by Francesco Cazzaniga and his brother Tommaso and Benedetto Briosco (1486). The second, the *Torelli Chapel*, was built in 1424. The

Church of Sant'Eustorgio, inside

statue of *St. Dominic* on the altar is by Carlo Rainoldi (1736) and the relief on the altar-front is by the same artist. On the left wall, *Sepulcher of Pietro Torelli* (died 1412), admirably sculpted by a Campionese master-carver. The frescoes on the walls are by Giovanni Mauro Fiammenghino. The third chapel was rebuilt in the Baroque style in the 18th century by Francesco Croce, and the restored *Sarcophagus of Protaso Caimi*, by Bonino da Campione (around

Church of Sant'Eustorgio, a dismantled triptych with the Madonna and Child between Saint James and Saint Augustine, by Bergognone (first chapel)

1360) has been placed against the left wall. Above, *St. Ambrose on Horseback* by Ambrogio Figino. On the right wall, an 18th century altarpiece with the *Madonna and Dominican Saints*. The fourth chapel, of the *Viscontis*, contains the *Mausoleum of Stefano Visconti* (died 1327) and his wife *Valentina Doria* (died 1359) by Giovanni di Balduccio da Pisa and by Bonino da Campione who remade the sarcophagus for Visconti's wife after her death. On the wall, above the mausoleum is the masterpiece of a Lombard Master of the 14th century, *Saint George and the Princess*. The frescoes on the vault and on the left wall are also by Lombard masters of the 14th century. Beneath the frescoes, a lovely *Crucifix* upon wood, by an Emilian Master of the beginning of the 14th century. In the fifth chapel on the altar, *Madonna and Child with Saints*, attributed to Cerano. In the sixth chapel, which belonged to the cadet branch of the Visconti family, to the right, *Tomb of Gaspare Visconti* (died 1434) probably by a Rhenish master of the early 15th century. To the left, *Tomb of Umberto Visconti*, with bas-reliefs on the sarcophagus and a *Pietà* (above) by Bonino da Campione. Underneath, inscription from the tomb with the reclining figure of *Agnese Besozzi* the second wife of Gaspare Visconti, by Ia-

Church of Sant'Eustorgio, Crucifix by an Emilian master (fourth chapel)

copino da Tradate (1420). In the seventh chapel, of the *Torriani Family*, there are 15th century frescoes in the vault which were restored in the 1950s and 1960s. In the right transept, above the two arches to the left, there is a fresco of the *Adoration of the Magi* attributed to Luini; from this point the visitor may

Church of Sant'Eustorgio, the Massacre of the Innocents by Cristoforo Storer

enter the *Chapel of the Magi* which contains the great Roman sarcophagus, in which the relics presumed to be of the three Magi were kept until 1164 when they were taken to Cologne. Above the altar is a three part reredos with bas-reliefs depicting episodes from the *Stories of the Three Kings*, by a 14th century master from the Po-valley area. In the presbytery, above the main altar is a great marble reredos divided into panels, with *Stories of the Passion*, a masterpiece by various artists of different periods starting in the beginning of the 14th century. Below the altar is an urn containing the remains of three Milanese bishops, *St. Eustorgius, St. Magnus* and *St. Honoratus.* Behind the altar, *Angels and Saints*, a fresco by Gaudenzio Ferrari. From the presbytery one enters the pseudo-crypt, erected in 1537 for which the 15th century columns from the adjoining Dominican cloister were used. The frescoes on the walls, representing *Procession of Saints* and the *Legend of the Seven Sleepers* are by Lombard painters of the 16th century. To the right we enter a chapel, built in 1575; on the left we can walk along a wide corridor with cross-vaulted ceilings where a 13th century multi-colored stone statue of *St. Eugene* is placed. The door to the left leads into the **Sacristy**, with its beautiful 17th century inlaid wardrobes. The corridor leads to a room which serves as a vestibule to the Portinari chapel opposite, and to the two 14th century Gothic chapels on the sides. The chapel on the right with its cross-vaulted ceiling, has a fresco on the wall by a 15th century Lombard master showing *Jesus, St. Dominic and a Devotee* as well as *St. Francis* by Chignoli. In the chapel to the left are the remains of frescoes by Daniele Crespi and

Church of Sant'Eustorgio, Madonna of the Milk by an anonymous Lombard painter of the 15th century

Madonna and Child by a 15th century painter. Through the archway flanked by two bronze candelabra one enters the Tuscan style **Portinari Chapel** dedicated to St. Peter Martyr, an early Renaissance architectural jewel.
The noble Florentine Pigello Portinari had the chapel built in 1462 while he was the procurator of the Medici Bank and the chapel was intended as a shrine for the remains of St. Peter Martyr and as a tomb for himself. It has not been ascertained who the builder was, but it is generally attributed to the Florentine architect Michelozzo Michelozzi, to whom Portinari had given the task of decorating the Milanese branch of the Medici bank that same year. The interior is a square surmounted by a circular dome and a niche-like chamber for the altar. A procession of angels bearing garlands in colored stucco by a Lombard decorator upon designs by a Tuscan master runs around the cylindrical drum, against a background of elegant little arches. The cycle of frescoes with the *Annunciation*, the *Assumption* and *Episodes from the Life*

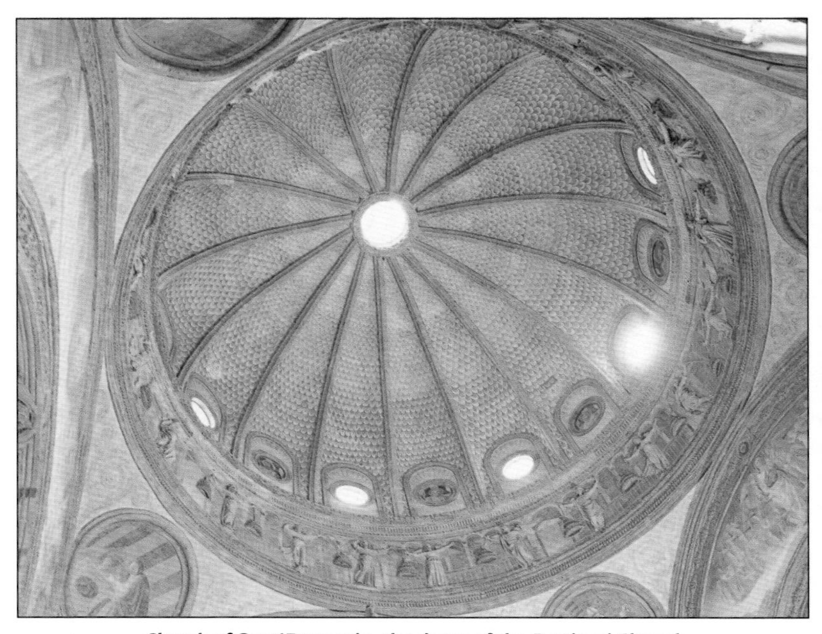

Church of Sant'Eustorgio, the dome of the Portinari Chapel

of St. Peter Martyr which decorate the chapel, is a masterpiece by Vincenzo Foppa, a great 15th century Lombard artist, who painted it in 1468. The celebrated *Tomb of St. Peter Martyr* sculpted by Giovanni di Balduccio da Pisa between 1336 and 1339 is in the center of the chapel and contains the remains of the Saint. The sarcophagus in white marble decorated with bas-reliefs representing *Episodes from the Life of the Saint*, is supported by eight columns flanked by eight statues symbolizing the *Virtues*. The sarcophagus, with a cover in the form of a truncated pyramid, is surmounted by a three-pointed shrine containing the statues of the *Madonna and Child between St. Dominic and St. Peter Martyr*. Inside the small chapel, to the left of the altar-chamber, the skull of the Saint is kept in a precious silver tabernacle.

Returning to the presbytery one turns down the left aisle, the chapels of which contain detached frescoes of the 13th - 15th centuries . In the seventh chapel a *Deposition* by Camillo Procaccini; in

Church of Sant'Eustorgio, the Tomb of Saint Peter Martyr in the Portinari Chapel

Porta Ticinese,
near the Basilica of San Lorenzo

the fifth chapel, *Monument of G. P. Varisio* of the 15th century and *Tombstone of the Bishop Federico Maggi* (died 1333) by a Campionese artist.

Basilica of San Lorenzo Maggiore

Sixteen fluted **columns** from a 2nd or 3rd century Roman building were moved here in the 4th century to form the pronaos of the great porticoed courtyard in front of the basilica. They represent the most significant remains of Roman and Early Christian Mediolanum. The bronze statue of the

Statue of Constantine,
located in the plaza in front
of the Basilica of San Lorenzo

Roman columns forming the great portico in front of the Basilica of San Lorenzo

Basilica of San Lorenzo seen from Piazza Vetra

Emperor Constantine which is a copy of the one in Rome, stands in the center of the courtyard. From Milan, in 313, Constantine issued his famous Edict granting the Christians religious freedom. The basilica was constructed towards the middle of the 4th century, as the Arian cathedral of Milan and became a Catholic church in the 5th century. Architecturally, the structure is an example of the old, majestic, central plan construction, typical of early

Basilica of San Lorenzo, façade

western Christianity. It was damaged by devastating fires in the 11th and 12th centuries and was restored in the Romanesque period; when part of the structure collapsed in the 16th century, San Carlo Borromeo had it substantially restored by Martino Bassi who added the cupola (1574) but kept the original, centrally oriented plan with its four corner turrets. The modern porticoed façade is by Cesare Nava (1894).

Basilica of San Lorenzo Maggiore, Chapel of S. Aquilino

Interior - It is solemn and majestic with its great dome and the four deep-set exedrae and has a wide walk-way sur-

Basilica of San Lorenzo Maggiore, detail of mosaics in the Chapel of S. Aquilino

mounted by the *matronei* or women's galleries which is reminiscent of the church of San Vitale in Ravenna. On the right, traces of Romanesque pilasters are visible and, after the first chapel, we find the square atrium with two apses with traces of 4th century mosaics and a fresco of the 14th century representing the *Crucifixion* and figures of *Saints*. Through a Roman door of the 1st century A.D. one enters the **Chapel of St. Aquilinus** which was built at the same time as the main church and still maintains its 4th century architectural characteristics. It is octagonal with niches, women's galleries (matronei) and is covered by a cupola. In the two end-niches there are Roman Christian mosaics of the 4th century depicting *Jesus between the Apostles* and a fragmentary scene of *Elijah in his Fiery Chariot*. In the other niches are Early Christian sarcophagi, including the 5th century one on the right, which according to tradition held the remains of Galla Placidia. The fresco of the *Pietà* in the lunette of the archway at the entrance is attributed to Bergognone. A staircase leads to the matroneo which is decorated with 4th century frescoes. From the chapel at the bottom, with the *Silver Tomb* containing the body of St. Aquilinus, one descends into the vast crypt built in part with stone blocks from a Roman building of the 2nd century. Returning to the church, on the wall, near the entrance to the chapel the visitor can admire a 13th century fresco of the *Deposition from the Cross*. Continuing, we pass under the tower with frescoes on the pillar and to the right the *Tomb of the Robiani* of the 15th century. Further ahead lies the **Cittadini Chapel** which has Romanesque origins with 15th century Gothic addi-

tions. Here we can see the remains of 13th century frescoes, and behind the altar, a 15th century triptych in bas-relief. Behind the main altar we find the **Chapel of St. Hippolytus** which was built in the 4th century. The interior is in the form of a Greek cross and the columns at the corners come from a building of the Imperial Roman epoch. Under the tower that follows, the *Tomb of Giovanni del Conte,* by Marco d'Agrate and Vincenzo Seregni. Next comes the **Chapel of St. Sixtus** preceded by a small atrium. It was constructed in the 5th century and has an octagonal interior with 17th century frescoes on the vault by Storer. Further on is an old fresco which is a reproduction of the *Last Supper* by Leonardo.

Church of Santa Maria della Passione

The construction of this vast building was begun towards the end of the 15th century by G. Battagio who designed it in the form of a Greek cross. The great cupola was completed in 1530. Towards the end of the 16th century, M.Bassi was given the task of enlarging the church and made additions to the front so that it was transformed into a Latin cross. The Baroque façade which is adorned with statues and reliefs is by the Barnabite friar, G.Rusnati, who completed it in 1729.

Interior - It is in the form of a Latin cross, has a main nave with three aisles

Church of Santa Maria della Passione, façade

Church of Santa Maria della Passione, inside

divided by pillars. Busts of *Saints* and *Members of the Lateran Order* painted on canvas by Daniele Crespi are hung at the base of the pillars. Beautiful 16th and 17th century paintings are to be found in the side and transept chapels. In the third chapel to the right, the *Offertory* by Daniele Crespi and the *Crowning with Thorns* by Cerano. In the fifth chapel the visitor can admire the 16th century fresco donated by the founder, Archbishop Daniele Birago, showing the *Madonna of the Passion*, which gave the church its name. In the sixth chapel *Madonna of Caravaggio* by Bramantino. At the base of the half columns beneath the vast octagon of the cupola, are paintings by Daniele Crespi with *Scenes of the Passion*. In the chapel of the right transept, on the altar, *Deposition* by Bernardino Luini (1516); on the right wall *Jesus among the Apostles* a fragment of a polyptych perhaps by Bergognone; the frescoes of the apse with the *Madonna at the Sepulcher* and "*Noli me tangere*" and those on the vault with the *Prophets* and *Evangelical Scenes* are by Antonio Campi. Under the organ in the niche to the right of the presbytery, *Funeral Monument of the Archbishop Daniele Birago*, founder of the church, by Andrea Fusina (1495). In the sacristy, on the walls and in the upper lunettes, frescoes by Bergognone. In the apse, 16th century inlaid wooden choir stalls, two paintings on canvas by Francesco Lanfranco with *Resurrection* and *Ascension* and frescoes by Nuvolone in the half-vault showing the *Coronation of Mary* and *Evangelists and Sibyls* on the ceiling-vault. On the altar of the chapel in the left transept *Last Supper*, by Gaudenzio Ferrari (1543); on the wall *Crucifixion* by Giulio Campi. In the chapel along the left aisle, various interesting paintings, including Daniele Crespi's *San Carlo* fasting in the first chapel. In the adjacent **Museo della Basilica** (Museum of the Basilica) which was started in the 1970s, we can find on display paintings of the Lombard school of the 17th century and objects related to the history of the church.

Church of Santa Maria at San Satiro

The church was founded by Bishop Ansperto in 876. It was a small church built on a piece of ground belonging to his family. The reconstruction was begun in 1478 by Bramante who added the octagonal sacristy which today is the baptistery. The façade which was begun by Amadeo in 1486 upon a design by Bramante, was left unfinished and was given its mod-

ern appearance by Giuseppe Vandoni in 1871. The bas-reliefs made by Amadeo, which were intended for placement in the roundels, are now kept in the Castello Sforzesco. The exterior of the apse is interesting, with its two portals opening out on the 15th century Chapel of the Pietà, cylindrical in form with niches and an octagonal drum. The 11th century campanile rises beside it and represents a veritable prototype for Lombard bell-towers.
The **interior**, notwithstanding the modest proportions of the church, is nobly spacious and admirably proportioned. It has three aisles, divided by pillars and a transept. The splendid coffered dome rises above the point at which the vaults of the transept and main nave meet. Behind the main altar, a series of vaulted pilasters in stucco designed by Bramante creates the illusion of a deep apse. At the end of the left arm of the transept, one enters the **Chapel of the Pietà**, which has maintained most of its original 9th century structure. Above the altar in the niche is a *Deposition* composed of 14 figures in colored terracotta, by Agostino de Fondutis (1483). To the right of the entrance, *Saints* and *Madonna and Child*, 10th century Byzantine style frescoes. From the right aisle, one enters the **Sacristy** or **Baptistery**, designed by Bramante, with its elegant octagonal form with two levels of loggias and a dome. The *Putti, Angels* and the *Male Busts* which form the frieze along the top, are in colored terracotta by Agostino de Fondutis based on models by Bramante.

Church of Santa Maria at San Satiro, inside

Church of Santa Maria at San Celso

The sanctuary is preceded by a large elegant atrium with porticos (1513) flanked by the remains of the old church of St. Celsus built in the 10th century, and a massive 13th century Romanesque bell-tower. The construction of the church of Santa Maria was begun in 1493 by the architect Gian Giacomo Dolcebuono after which Cristofaro Solari and Giovanni Antonio Amadeo took over and finished in 1505. In 1513 Cesariano was asked to enlarge the church, but he only completed the porticoed atrium, while the interior was modified by Cristoforo Lombardo and finished by Vincenzo Seregni in 1563. The façade, begun in 1565 by Galeazzo Alessi and

Church of Santa Maria at San Celso

finished by his successor Martino Bassi, is divided into four registers and surmounted by a tympanum. We can see the statues of *Adam and Eve* in the niches of the lower register, and, along the sides of the three portals, the *Angel*, the *Virgin of the Annunciation* and the relief above the central portal by Stoldo Lorenzi: the *Sybil* on the portal, the four *Prophets* in the side niches, the *Angels with the Madonna* (a copy) in the tympanum and the bas-reliefs are by Annibale Fontana. The polygonal drum with the series of biforus windows is by Dolcebuono.

The **interior** is a Latin cross with three aisles supported by pillars, a great barrel vault with dome and presbytery surrounded by a walkway. Besides the beautiful 16th century decorations (note the handsome gilded coffered vaults) the church boasts many beautiful works of art. The niches at the bottom of the columns which support the cupola in the central nave contain, to the left, a statue of the *Baptist* and to the right a statue of *Elijah*, both by Stoldo Lorenzi. At the next column, we find a statue of *St. John the Evangelist* by Annibale Fontana and below, an epigraph dedicated to the artist who is buried here. *Altar of the Madonna* by Martino Bassi at the opposite column with a statue of the *Assumption* by Fontana (1586), who also made the bronze candelabrum left of the main altar. In the fourth Chapel of the right aisle: *Martyrdom of St. Nazarius and St. Celsus*, by Cesare Procaccini (1607). On the altar of the right transept, *Holy Family* and *St. Jerome* by Paris Bordone. The arches along the walk way contain a series of paintings on canvas, which in-

Church of Santa Maria at San Celso, detail of the façade

clude, in the fourth arch, *Baptism of Jesus* by Gaudenzio Ferrari and in the seventh, *Conversion of St. Paul* by Moretto da Brescia. The altar at the end of the left transept is composed of a *sarcophagus* of the 4th century, containing the body of St. Celsus, placed there by St. Ambrose. In the third chapel of the left aisle, *Martyrdom of St. Catherine* by Cerano (1603); in the first chapel, *Madonna adoring the Child* by Bergognone. Above the portal, statue of the *Madonna* by Annibale Fontana, which was originally on the façade, and has now been substituted by a copy. The Treasure Sacristy used to contain the so-called *Chiaravalle Processional Cross* in red jasper, gold and gems, which has now been removed to another place for safekeeping, and an amphora of gilded silver, attributed to Benvenuto Cellini, together with chalices, relics, monstrances etc.

Church of San Carlo al Corso

The church dedicated to San Carlo was designed by Carlo Amati between 1832 and 1847, and built on the site of the pre-existing church of Santa Maria dei Servi. It has a Corinthian pronaos flanked by porticos. Architecturally it is a central plan construction covered by a dome, supported by Corinthian columns and erected without re-enforcement, by Felice Pizzagalli; niche-like chapels are built between the Corinthian columns.

In the third chapel to the right *Deposition*, by Pompeo Marchesi ordered by Ferdinand and Francis I of Austria; in the third chapel to the left, *St. Charles giving Holy Communion to St. Luigi Gonzaga* by Marchesi.

Church of San Carlo al Corso, façade

The Lazzaretto

After its demolition in 1882 only a part of the portico in Via San Gregorio remains today of the old Lazzaretto mentioned by Manzoni. The remains give some idea of the great building which covered a square area marked-off by Via San Gregorio, Via Lazzaretto, Viale Vittorio Veneto and Corso Buenos Aires as they are today. It was planned by the "Captains and Defenders of the city of Milan" as a hospital to isolate and heal the plague-stricken inhabitants at the time of the Ambrosian Republic (1447). The construction of the building under the direction of Lazzaro Palazzi, went on until 1513. Three sides of the portico lead into 228 little cells; in the center stood a small church which was rebuilt by order of Bishop Carlo Borromeo after the plague of 1576, and was renamed **San Carlo al Lazzaretto** (in Via Lecco).

The Lazzaretto

Church of San Nazaro Maggiore

The church was founded in the 4th century by St. Ambrose who had the remains of St. Nazarius transferred there. The original outside walls of the church have survived, but the rest was rebuilt in the 11th century. Of these structures the 11th century apse remains, but most of the rest was remodeled during one of the many later alterations.

The **interior** of the church is preceded by the **Funeral Chapel of the Trivulzio Family**, octagonal in form, with a cupola constructed in 1512 by Bramantino, commissioned by Marshall Gian Giacomo Trivulzio. In the niches are eight tombs with reclining statues of members of the *Trivulzio family.* The one in front of the entrance is the *Sarcophagus of Gian Giacomo Trivulzio,* sculpted by Francesco Brioso, which bears the

Church of S. Nazaro Maggiore, façade

Church of S. Nazaro Maggiore, Trivulzio funeral chapel

famous Latin inscription “Qui numquam quievit quiescit: tace” (he who never found peace now rests: silence). The interior of the church is in the form of a Greek cross with a great dome and a deep apse. The 15th century fresco on the altar on the left wall shows *Madonna and Child and St. Matronianus* and a 13th century frescoed *Christ appearing to Mary Magdalene* is at the same altar. In the right transept, in the niche, *Last Supper*, a copy by Lanino of the work by Gaudenzio Ferrari. Opposite the *Altar of St. Matronianus* and on the wall, a bas-relief with a *Crucifixion* by Bonino da Campione. From the right of the presbytery one enters the small 10th century *Chapel of St. Linus.* From the left transept, one enters the **Chapel of St. Catherine**, built in 1540, with a large fresco reproducing the *Martyrdom of St. Catherine*, by Lanino (1546).

Church of S. Nazaro Maggiore, inside

Church of San Simpliciano

This is one of the oldest churches in Milan. It was founded by St. Ambrose in the 4th century and constructed, it is believed, upon the site of an ancient pagan cemetery. It was then completed by St. Simplicianus who was buried here. The alterations and reconstruction over the centuries, have obliterated the original shape, as the walls of the Early Christian building have been almost completely incorporated into the later

Church of San Simpliciano, façade

structures. Of the façade, which was restored in 1870, only the middle portal is old (12th century); the capitals adorned with figures represent the *Processions of the Wise Virgins and the Foolish Virgins.*

The **interior**, with three naves, still has visible traces, especially on the walls of the nave, of the Early Christian construction. Several paintings by artists of the 16th and 17th century are worthy of note. On the altar of the third chapel of the right aisle, *St. Benedict* by Enea Salmeggia. Beneath the organ pipes, which are in the presbytery, are figures of *Saints* by Aurelio Luini. In the half-vault of the apse, a great fresco executed by Bergognone, around 1515 of the *Coronation of Mary*, a magnificent composition with the *Holy Father receiving Jesus and the Madonna in His Arms*, surrounded by a circle of *Angels* and *Saints.*

The Naviglio Canal

The Canal was built in 1177, when the city was given new walls. This canal, which is fed by the Adda and the Ticino rivers, was intended for irrigation purposes, and to make the various water mills along the banks work; in addition it channeled the rivulets and streams flowing in the vicinity of the town, giving rise to the network of canals which exists today. This network centers on the *Naviglio Grande*, which comes from the Ticino and which was made navigable in 1269 for the transport of the marble required for the construction of the cathedral. After the Naviglio, the *Pavia Canal* was built, to provide water for the park of the Castle of Pavia; next came the picturesque *Martesana Canal* which channeled the waters of the Adda and which led to the building of the wharf at the Ticino Gate (Darsena di Porta Ticinese).

The Naviglio canal

Porta Ticinese

The Main Hospital Cà Granda

The Ospedale Maggiore (Main Hospital), known to the Milanese as *Cà Granda* came into being when it was decided to house the thirty or so hospitals in the area of Corso di Porta Romana in a single unified structure. It was founded by Francesco Sforza in 1456 and the first construction phase lasted until 1497 when Filarete, Solari and Amadeo, worked on the quadrilateral towards San Nazaro; the second phase started in 1624 when the central part of the façade, the courtyard and the church were built, under the direction of the architects F. M. Richini, G. B. Pessina, F. Mangone and Cerano; the third phase lasted from 1794 to 1804 when the internal courtyard of the second cross-section and the third side of the façade were built by the engineer P. Castelli. The building was terribly damaged by the 1943 bombings and then reconstructed. It now houses the *Rectors'offices*, the *Schools of Literature* and *Philosophy* and the *Law School* of the **State University.**

The Main Hospital

Useful Information

Useful information

Foreword

For a great city like Milan it is impossible to list in such a brief space all of the facilities, institutions, businesses and activities in some way related to, or intended to assist, tourists. For this reason the lists of names and addresses represents simply a random selection made by the editor and in no way constitutes a negative opinion towards those activities or businesses whose names are not mentioned in this guide book.

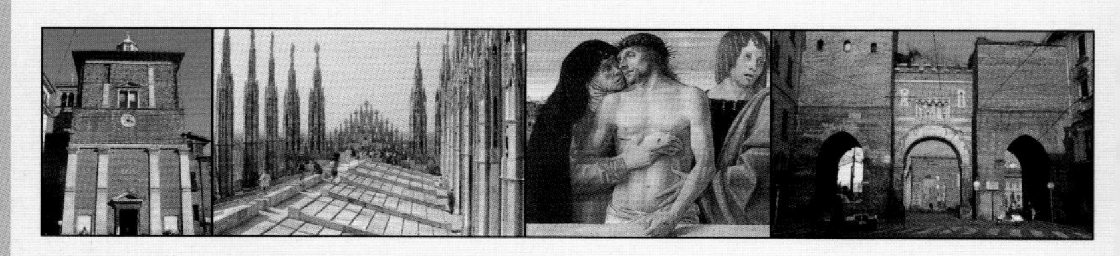

By Car

Milan is located in the geographic center of the great plain of the Po valley and has excellent connections with the major expressways running through Northern Italy both in an East-West direction (from the Piedmont and Aosta Valley regions to Friuli and Venezia Giulia) as well as in a North-South direction (toward Switzerland, Liguria and Emilia-Romagna). Of these, the most important express way is the **A1**, the principal artery connecting **Northern and Southern Italy**, which is called the Autostrada del Sole or the Milano-Napoli; exit at **Milano Sud**. The **A4** expressway is the main East-West artery and connects Torino to Trieste; it has exits for Milan at **Milano-Ghisolfa** and **Milano Est**. The **A8** expressway goes from Milan to Varese and its branch, the **A9**, leads to the Lake district and Switzerland (exit **Milano Nord**); The A7 expressway connects Milan to Genova; exit at Milano. Another important access road to Milan, is the **SS. 33** coming from Spluga, which, up to the point where the river Adda flows into the Lario, has all of the characteristics of a super highway. Milan is surrounded by a vast network of ring roads (tangenziali) from which one can exit to reach the main access roads leading to the dowtown area. The **Tangenziale Ovest** on the West receives all of the traffic coming from Piedmont and Liguria, while the **Tangenziale Est** on the East receives automobile traffic coming from the South on the Autostrada del Sole, and from the main cities to the East like Brescia, Verona (Brennero), Venice and Trieste

By Airplane

Starting in October of 1998, the major volume of both national and international air traffic has been directed to the intercontinental airport of **Malpensa 2000**. This new airport with its remarkable and efficient complex of facilities is the result of a vast project of enlargement, remodeling and modernization of the old Malpensa airport. Malpensa 2000 is located 46 km. Northwest of Milan. Since October of 1999 it has had direct train connections with the main railway station in downtown Milan. The airport can also be reached by a direct bus service which departs from the main Milan station in Via Lampugnano as well as from the Line 1 subway station in Via Lampugnano; the trip to the airport takes about 60 minutes.

The second airport of Milan is **Linate**, which received a large portion of the domestic air traffic before the renovation of the Malpensa airport. This airport is also called the Forlanini airport and is located just 5 km. East of the city. It is connected to the downtown area by a bus service which leaves from the railway station. There is also a municipal bus service which connects Linate to downtown Milan, A.T.M. bus no. 73, which leaves from Piazza San Babila and reaches Linate in about 35 minutes.

By Train

The Milanese train station is the most important in Northern Italy and Milan has excellent railway connections with the main lines to all other Italian and foreign cities. The main lines of the Eurostar and other high-speed trains arrive at the **Central Station** and from the station it is easy to reach both the subway (lines 2 and 3) and the city buses. **Porta Garibaldi** and **Lambrate** are also important secondary train stations and are both located on Line 2 of the subway; also, **Porta Genova, Porta Romana, Porta Vittoria**. The station of **Ferrovie Nord** which is located in Piazza Cadorna on Lines 1 and 2 of the subway, serves travelers going to and from the Lake District and Brianza.

By Bus

There are numerous bus services connecting Milan to the other major cities of Lombardy. There are also excellent connections to cities outside of the region and to tourist attractions and recreational areas. Most of these services are organized and run by tour operators or travel agencies.

INFORMATION

☎ 02; ✉ 20100
(see also the list of postal codes for the city)

INFORMATION OFFICE

International Milan Fair
Largo Domodossola, 1
☎ 02/485501 - Fax 02/48004423
Provincial Tourist Office for the greater Milan area - Via Marconi, 1
☎ 02/809662 - Fax 02/72022999
Autonomous Organization for the International Milan Fair
Largo Domodossola, 1
☎ 02/49971 - Fax 02/4997

INFORMATION OFFICE FOR TRANSPORTATION

Milanese Transportation Company (ATM)
Foro Bonaparte, 61
☎ 02/8055841

FOR TRAIN INFORMATION

Central Station
Piazza Duca d'Aosta ☎ 02/675001
Porta Garibaldi Station
Piazza Freud ☎ 02/6552078
Lambrate Station
Piazza Bottini ☎ 02/67711
Northern Milan Railways
Piazzale Cadorna ☎ 02/8511608

FOR AIRPORT INNFORMATION

Airports of Milan (SEA)
☎ 02/74851-Fax 02/74852010
Malpensa Airport
☎ 02/74852200
Alitalia ☎ 02/40099240
Linate Airport
☎ 02/74852200
Alitalia ☎ 02/24991

FOR TAXI INFORMATION

Taxi Malpensa 2000 ☎ 02/40099029
S. Ambrogio Radio Taxi Data ☎ 5353
Autoradiotassi ☎ 8585
Cooperativa Esperia ☎ 02/8321084
Cooperativa Italiana Taxi
☎ 02/48700207

Cooperativa Tassisti Città di Milano
☎ 02/8263895
Cooperativa Tassisti Associati
☎ 02/3450357
La Base A.S.T.L.A. ☎ 02/26666022
Pronto Taxi ☎ 02/57419128
Taxi Piazza Lega Lombarda
☎ 02/313616
Taxi Piazza Sempione ☎ 02/342132
Taxi Piazza Bottini ☎ 02/2364375
Taxi Corso Lodi ☎ 02/5469092
Taxi Corso Buenos Aires ☎ 02/201770
Taxi Piazzale Lotto ☎ 02/4695119
Taxi Piazza Duomo ☎ 02/86462013

Bicycle Rental

La Bicycletta
Via Pisanello, 26 ☎ 02/4072396

Automobile Rental

Frigerio Viaggi - Via C.Poerio, 29
☎ 02/29514647 - Fax 02/29513952
Avis - Piazza Diaz, 6 ☎ 02/863494
Avis - Malpensa 2000 ☎ 02/40099375
Avis - Linate ☎ 02/717214
Maggiore - Stazione Centrale
☎ 02/6690934
Maggiore - Malpensa 2000
☎ 02/40099330
Maggiore - Linate ☎ 02/717210
Vip Limousine - Via Bonnet, 6
☎ 02/6592158
Auto Europa - Via Tunisia, 23
☎ 02/29403525
Autonoleggio Tirreno - Via Lepetit, 31
☎ 02/6694011
Italauto - Via Corelli, 56
☎ 02/70200393
Travelcar ☎ 02/313178
Eurocar - Gall. Sala dei Longobardi, 2
☎ 02/86462641
Europcar ☎ 02/70399700
Hertz Italiana - Via Progresso, 3
☎ 02/67073236
Sixt - Via Boccaccio, 21
☎ 02/468348
Sixt - Malpensa 2000 ☎ 02/40099481
Sixt - Linate ☎ 02/70200266

Garages

Autosilo della Moscova
Via Moscova,47 ☎ 02/6570049
Autosilo di Porta Nuova
Via S. Marco, 28 ☎ 02/6570114
Mascagni Parking
Via Mascagni, 6 ☎ 02/794600
Statuto Parking
Via Statuto, 21 ☎ 02/6555525
Ambrosiano
Via Bazzini, 16 ☎ 02/2666219
Autogarage Bottego
Via Bottego, 15 ☎ 02/2564779
Central Parking
Via Lepetit, 8/10 ☎ 02/66484709
Fergo
Via Gozzi, 5 ☎ 02/7383443
Mediolanum
Via Copernico, 55 ☎ 02/67075215
Città Parcheggio
Via Rogoredo, 128 ☎ 02/510445
Porta Romana
Viale Monte Nero, 16a ☎ 02/59901389
Sea Parking
Via Forlanini ☎ 02/7561258
Città Parcheggio
Via Lorenteggio, 208a ☎ 02/4150656
Internazionale
Via Valparaiso, 8 ☎ 02/4812109
Fiera
Viale Cassiodoro, 26 ☎ 02/48014118
Nord Milano
Corso Sempione, 23 ☎ 02/312026

Autosilo Bassidue
Via U. Bassi, 6 ☎ 02/6081233
New Parking Principe
Via Principe Eugenio, 12 ☎ 02/315389

Parking

Like all great cities, Milan has major problems with automobile traffic. It is not easy to find a place to park in the city, and the downtown is closed to all automobile traffic except for residents. Automobiles with license plates from other provinces or countries can try to find parking spaces in the expensive metered parking zones; in order to do this drivers must buy the **"Scratch and Park Cards" (gratta e sosta)**, scratch off the date and time of arrival, and display the card on the dashboard in the windshield. It is certainly preferable to leave the car outside of the downtown area, i.e., beyond the circle of the Navigli and come into town using public transportation, or else leave your car at one of the parking lots provided at the suburban subway stations. These are, for **Line 1**, at Molino Dorino, Lampugnano, Bisceglie, Sesto Marelli; for **Line 2** at Cologno, Gessate, Cascina Gobba, Crescenzago, and Romolo; and for **Line 3**, at the stations of Rogoredo and San Donato.

Emergency Telephone numbers

Police/Public assistance:
Emergency ☎ 113
State Police (Questura)
Via Fatebenefratelli, 11 ☎ 02/62261
Highway Police
Via Jacopino da Tradate, 1 ☎ 02/326781
Carabinieri (Federal Police) ☎ 112
Carabinieri- Via Marcora, 1 ☎ 02/62761
Medical Emergency:
Ambulance ☎ 118
Doctor on call ☎ 02/34567
Cardiological emergency
☎ 02/89406035/6
Poison antidote treatment ☎ 02/66101029
Burn treatment ☎ 02/64442625
Croce d'Oro
Piazzale Ferrara, 4 ☎ 02/57402525
Croce Rosa-Celeste
Via Castelvetro, 32 ☎ 02/3319845
Croce Verde Musocco
Piazzale S. Santarosa, 10
☎ 02/38006468
Croce Verde Sempione
Piazzale S. Santarosa, 10
☎ 02/38006477
Ente Ospedaliero Niguarda Ca' Granda
Centro Antiveleno
Piazza Ospedale Maggiore, 3
☎ 02/66101029
Ente Ospedaliero Ospedale
Fatebenefratelli e Oftalmico
Corso P.ta Nuova, 23 ☎ 02/63631
European School of Oncology
Via Ripamonti, 436 ☎ 02/57410245
Fatebenefratelli
C.so P.ta Nuova, 23 ☎ 02/6572898
02/29017027 - 02/29017028
02/29017029

Fondazione Centro San Raffaele del Monte Tabor
Via Olgettina, 60 ☎ 02/26431
Fondazione P.J. Don C. Gnocchi
Via Capecelatro, 66 ☎ 02/403081
Generale Provinciale Ente Ospedaliero S. Carlo Borromeo
Via Pio II, 3 ☎ 02/40221
Generale Regionale Ente Ospedaliero Niguarda Ca' Granda
Piazza Ospedale Maggiore, 3 ☎ 02/64441
Istituto di Ostetrica-Ginecologia e Pediatria Regina Elena
Via Fanti, 6 ☎ 02/5516352 - 02/57911
Istituto Nazionale per la Cura e lo Studio dei Tumori
Via Venezian, 1 ☎ 02/2367412
Istituto Neurologico Carlo Besta
Via Celoria, 11 ☎ 02/23941
Istituto Ortopedico Gaetano Pini
Piazza Ferrari, 1 ☎ 02/582961
Maggiore di Milano
Via Sforza, 35 ☎ 02/55180005
Maggiore di Milano
Via Lamarmora, 5 ☎ 02/55188962
Niguarda
Piazza Ospedale Maggiore, 3
☎ 02/66102206
San Giovanni di Dio
Via Esopo, 7 ☎ 02/27002336
San Raffaele
Via S. Croce, 10 ☎ 02/581871
ACI (Italian Automobil Club) ☎ 116
Airport Malpensa 2000
☎ 02/74852200
Airport of Linate ☎ 02/74852200
Fire Department
emergency ☎ 115
Fire Department
Via Messina, 35-39 ☎ 02/3190501
Municipal Police
Piazza Beccaria, 19 ☎ 02/77271
Railway Police
Corso Magenta, 24 ☎ 02/86453156
State Railways Train information (Central Station) ☎ 02/675001
City Hall
Piazza della Scala, 2 ☎ 02/86453156
Tourist information ☎ 02/809662

Banks and Saving And Loan Institutions

Banca Commerciale Italiana
Piazza della Scala, 6
Banca di Roma
Via Lauro, 9
Banca d'Italia
Via Cordusio, 5
Banca Fideuram
Corso di Porta Romana, 16
Banca Mediolanum
Piazza De Angeli, 1
Banca Nazionale del Lavoro
Piazza S. Fedele, 1/3
Banca Nazionale dell'Agricoltura
Piazza Fontana, 4
Banca Popolare di Milano
Corso Buenos Aires, 36
Banca Toscana
Foro Bonaparte, 12/8
Banco Ambrosiano Veneto
Piazza P. Ferrari, 10
Banco di Napoli
Piazza Cordusio, 2
Banco di Sicilia
Via Massarani, 7
Carige
Piazzetta Pattari, 1
Cariplo
Via Ripamonti, 166
Istituto Bancario Italiano
Viale Monza, 14

Istituto Bancario San Paolo di Torino
Via Broletto, 9/11
Mediobanca
Via Filodrammatici, 10
Monte dei Paschi di Siena
Via S. Margherita, 11
Rolo Banca
Via Cordusio, 3
Unicredito Italiano
Piazza Cordusio

Agritourism Farms

Agriturismo Ca' del Conte
Cascina Ca' Del Conte
San Martino in Strada ☎ 0371/36291
Brambilla - Cascina Trecascine
Via Trecascine, 67 - Lodi
☎ 0371/424855 - Fax 0371/424855
Cascina Caremma
Via Cascina Caremma - Besate
☎ 02/9050020 - Fax 02/9050020
Di Leo
V.le Suzzani, 250 - Milano
☎ 02/6425845
In Mezzo Al Verde
Via Roma, 13 - Ozzero
☎ 02/9407436

Hotels

*****
Duca di Milano
Piazza della Repubblica, 13
☎ 02/62841 - Fax 02/6555966
Four Seasons - Via Gesù, 8
☎ 02/77088 - Fax 02/77085000
Grand Hotel et de Milan - Via Manzoni, 29
☎ 02/723141 - Fax 02/86460861
Palace - Piazza della Repubblica, 20
☎ 02/63361 - Fax 02/654485
Principe di Savoia
Piazza della Repubblica, 17
☎ 02/62301 - Fax ☎ 02/6595838

****
Ambasciatori - Galleria del Corso, 3
☎ 02/76020241 - Fax 02/782700
Carlton Senato - Via Senato, 5
☎ 02/76015535 - Fax 02/783300
Excelsior Gallia - Piazza Duca d'Aosta, 9
☎ 02/67851 - Fax 02/66713239
Grand Hotel Duomo - Via S. Raffaele, 1
☎ 02/8833 - Fax 02/86462027
Grand Hotel Fieramilano
Viale Boezio, 20
☎ 02/336221 - Fax 02/314119
Hilton - Via Galvani, 12
☎ 02/69831 - Fax 02/66710810

Holiday Inn Milan
Via Lorenteggio, 218
☎ 02/410014 - Fax 02/48304729
Ibis Ca' Granda - Viale Suzzani, 13/15
☎ 02/66103000 - Fax 02/66102797
Ibis Centro - Via Zarotto, 8
☎ 02/6315 - Fax 02/6598026
Jolly President - Largo Augusto, 10
☎ 02/77461 - Fax 02/783449
Jolly Touring - Via Tarchetti, 2
☎ 02/6335 - Fax ☎ 02/6592209
Leonardo da Vinci - Via Senigallia, 6
☎ 02/64071 - Fax 02/64074839
Novotel Milano Est Aeroporto
Via Mecenate, 121
☎ 02/58011085 - Fax 02/58011086
Novotel Milano Nord
Viale Suzzani, 13
☎ 02/66101861 -Fax 02/66101961
Raffaello - Viale Certosa, 108
☎ 02/3270446 - Fax 02/3270440
Royal Mercure - Via Cardano, 1
☎ 02/6709151 - Fax 02/6703024
Starhotel Ritz - Via Spallanzani, 40
☎ 02/2055 - Fax 02/29518679

***

Accursio - Viale Certosa, 88
☎ 02/33001270 - Fax 02/39217466
Admiral - Via Domodossola, 16
☎ 02/3492151 - Fax 02/33106660
Ambrosiano - Via S. Sofia, 9
☎ 02/58306044 - Fax 02/58305067
Ariosto - Via Ariosto, 22
☎ 02/4817844 - Fax 02/4980516
Astoria - Viale Murillo, 9
☎ 02/40090095 - Fax 02/40074642
Buenos Aires - Corso Buenos Aires, 26
☎ 02/29400169 - Fax 02/29402494
Canada - Via S. Sofia, 11
☎ 02/58304844 - Fax 02/58300282
City - Corso Buenos Aires, 42/5
☎ 02/29523382 - Fax 02/2046957
Gala - Viale Zara, 89/91
☎ 02/66800891 - Fax 02/66800463
Major - Viale Isonzo, 2
☎ 02/55188335 - Fax 02/55183140

Nuovo Biscione
Via S. M. Fulcorina, 15
☎ 02/8693656 - Fax 02/8056825
Park - Via Massena, 9
☎ 02/312525 - Fax 02/33103675
Roxy - Via Bixio, 4a
☎ 02/29525151 - Fax 02/29517627
Sant'Ambroeus - Viale Papiniano, 14
☎ 02/48008989 - Fax 02/48008687
Scala Nord - Via F. Ferruccio, 10a
☎ 02/316041 - Fax 02/33101473
Vittoria - Via P. Calvi, 32
☎ 02/5456520 - Fax 02/55190246

**

Adler - Via Ricordi, 10
☎ 02/29529795 - Fax 02/29526612
Apollo - Via Ripamonti, 102
☎ 02/5393446 - Fax 02/57303913
Boston - Via Lepetit, 7
☎ 02/6692636 - Fax 02/66981802
Cinque Giornate
Piazza Cinque Giornate, 6
☎ 02/5463433 - Fax 02/5513611
London - Via Rovello, 3
☎ 02/72020166 - Fax 02/8057037
Parma - Via Pier della Francesca, 48
☎ 02/315448 - Fax 02/315466
Vecchia Milano - Via Borromei, 4
☎ 02/875042 - Fax 02/86454292

*

Ambrosiana - Via Plinio, 22
☎ 02/2049670 - Fax 02/29529176
Arlecchino - Via Paganini, 7
☎ 02/29519859 - Fax 02/2047174
Brianza Via P. Castaldi, 16
☎ 02/29404819 - Fax 02/29531145
Capri - Viale dei Mille, 24
☎ 02/713694 - Fax 02/70105859
Manzoni - Via Senato, 45
☎ 02/76021002 - Fax 02/798834

Rental Agencies: Vacation Houses and Apartments

Contessa Jolanda - Via Murat, 21
☎ 02/69761 - Fax 02/66802368
Lepontina - Via Lepontina, 9
☎ 02/66802508 - Fax 02/66802703
Romana - Corso Porta Romana, 64
☎ 02/58309747 - Fax 02/58309448

Restaurants Cafes and Pizzerias

Agnello - Via Agnello, 8
☎ 02/86461654
Al Conte Ugolino - Piazza Beccaria, 6
☎ 02/876134
Al Dollaro Stef
Via Paolo da Cannobio, 11
☎ 02/804138
Al Porto - P.le Cantore
☎ 02/89407425
Al Vesuvio - Via Ausonio, 23
☎ 02/8394993
Alfio Cavour - Via Senato, 31
☎ 02/780731
Amì Berton - Via Nullo, 14
☎ 02/713669
Antica Trattoria Stomaco di Ferro
Via Osti,4 ☎ 02/877648
Antica Trattoria Triestina
Via S. Vittore, 13 ☎ 02/468355
Bandiere - Via Palermo, 15
☎ 02/86461646
Barbarossa da Flavio - Via Cerva, 10
☎ 02/781418
Biffi Scala e Toulà - Via Filodrammatici, 2
☎ 02/866651 - Fax 02/86461060
Bistrot di Gualtiero Marchesi
Via San Raffaele, 2
☎ 02/877120 - Fax 877035

Boeucc - Piazza Belgioioso, 2
☎ 02/76020224
Cantina Piemontese - Via Laghetto, 11
☎ 02/784618
Caruso del Grand Hotel et de Milan
Via Manzoni, 29 ☎ 02/72314
Casanova Grill dell'Hotel Palace
Piazza della Repubblica ☎ 02/29000803
Charleston - Piazza Liberty, 8
☎ 02/798631
Ciardi - Via San Raffaele, 6
☎ 02/877698
Cinque Terre - Via Andrea Appiani, 9
☎ 02/6575177
Colline Pisane - Largo La Foppa, 5
☎ 02/6599136
Dolly's - Via C.G. Merlo, 1 ☎ 02/798324
Down Town - Gall. Piazza Duomo
☎ 02/866907
Five - Corso Magenta, 78
☎ 02/48014159
Franco il Contadino - Via Fiori Chiari, 20
☎ 02/86463446
Fuori Orario - Via Festa del Perdono, 4
☎ 02/58307404
Galleria Meravigli
Via Negri, 6 - Via Meravigli, 3
☎ 02/8055125
Gargantua - Corso di P.ta Vigentina, 31
☎ 02/58314888
Genovese - Via E. Troilo,14
☎ 02/8373180
Greco - Corso di P.ta Ticinese, 76
☎ 02/58103862
Hippopotamus - Via dei Fabbri, 1
☎ 02/8379103
Il Duomo del Grand Hotel Duomo
Via S. Raffaele, 1 ☎ 02/8833
Infinito - Via Leopardi, 25
☎ 02/4692276
Langhe - Corso Como, 6
☎ 02/6554279
Longhi - Corso Italia, 46
☎ 02/58322169
Lo Scoglio - Piazza XXIV Maggio, 10
☎ 02/89403750
Lo Strapuntino - Corso Garibaldi, 17
☎ 02/8053160
L'Assassino - Via Amedei, 8
☎ 02/8056512
L'Ulmet
Via Disciplini ang. Via Olmetto
☎ 02/86452718
Malastrana Rossa
Corso Garibaldi, 50
☎ 02/86462074

Matarel - Corso Garibaldi, 75
☎ 02/654204
Mei Lin - Via S. G. sul Muro, 13
☎ 02/86450881
Mergellina - Via Molino Armi, 48
☎ 02/89401333
Mirabilia Restaurant Club
Via Festa del Perdono, 12 ☎ 02/58307408
Mythos - Via Vico, 4
☎ 02/48006010
Momus - Via Fiori Chiari, 8
☎ 02/8056227
Montecristo - Via Prina, 17
☎ 02/312760
Oasi della Pizza - Via San Maurilio, 2
☎ 02/86454619
Olivia - Via G. D' Annunzio, 7/9
☎ 02/89406052
Ostarìa Vècju Friûl - Via E. De Marchi, 5
☎ 02/6704295
Osteria del Laghetto
Via Festa del Perdono, 1 ☎ 02/76002992
Osteria dell' Operetta
C.so di P.ta Ticinese, 70 ☎ 02/89407426
Osteria della Lanterna - Via Mercalli, 3
☎ 02/58309604
Osteria Via Prè - Via Casale, 4
☎ 02/8373869
Pagni - Via Orti, 7
☎ 02/55011267
Pane & Farina - Via Pantano, 6
☎ 02/8693274
Paper Moon - Via Bagutta, 1
☎ 02/76022297
Peschereccio - Via Quintino Sella, 2
☎ 02/861418
Popeye - Via S. Tecla, 3
☎ 02/862715
Riccione - Via Taramelli, 70
☎ 02/6686807
Sadler Osteria di Porta Cicca
Ripa di Porta Ticinese, 1 ☎ 02/58104451
Saint Andrew's - Via Sant'Andrea, 23
☎ 02/76023132
Sant'Eustorgio - Piazza Sant'Eustorgio, 6
☎ 02/58101396
Savini - Galleria Vittorio Emanuele II
☎ 02/72003433
Solferino - Via Castelfidardo, 2
☎ 02/6599886
Solito Posto - Via Bruni, 13
☎ 02/6888310
Stendhal - Via San Marco ang. Via Ancona
☎ 02/6555587
Taverna della Trisa - Via F. Ferruccio, 1
☎ 02/341304
Taverna Morigi - Via Morigi, 8
☎ 02/86450880
Trattoria da Pino - Via Cerva, 14
☎ 02/76000532
Trattoria Milanese - Via Santa Marta, 11
☎ 02/86451991
Valtellina - Via Taverna, 34
☎ 02/7561139
Vecchia Napoli
Via S. Tommaso, 6
☎ 02/86462709

SELF SERVICES AND FAST - FOOD

Amico Motta - Via Orefici, 1
☎ 02/72002211
Autogrill - Piazza Duomo, 24
☎ 02/86467365
Charly Ristorante Self Service
Via Mecenate, 77 ☎ 02/5060382
Daniel's Restaurant - Via Corridoni, 22
☎ 02/55184861
Italian Break - Corso Italia, 13
☎ 02/89010882
Mc Donald's - Via De Amicis, 25
☎ 02/58100137

Mc Donald's
Largo Corsia Servi, 11
☎ 02/76008502
Mc Donald's - Piazza Duomo, 17
☎ 02/86460435
Mc Donald's - Via Durini, 27
☎ 02/780860
Mc Donald's - Via Foscolo, 3
☎ 02/86460065
Mc Donald's - Piazza Cordusio, 2
☎ 02/8055697
Milano Ciao - Corso Europa, 12
☎ 02/76024211

Coffee Bars and Pastry Shops

Atm Bar - Bastioni di Porta Volta, 15
☎ 02/6552365
Biffi - C.so Magenta, 87 ☎ 02/48006702
Boulevard Cafè - C.so Garibaldi, 39
☎ 02/72003435
Brunch di Gualtiero Marchesi
P.za Duomo, 1 ☎ 02/877159
Cafè du Bateau - P.le Cantore
☎ 02/89408266
Camparino
Gall. Vittorio Emanuele II, P.zza Duomo
☎ 02/86464435
Cap Saint Martin - Via De Amicis, 9
☎ 02/8394145
Carmel Cafè - Via Conca Naviglio, 37
☎ 02/8322621
Cavour - Via S. Maria alla Porta, 13
☎ 02/86454690
Cucchi - C.so Genova, 1
☎ 02/89409793
Daniel Bar
Via Crocefisso, 27 ang. Via della Chiusa
☎ 02/58313766
G.B. Bar - Via Agnello, 18
☎ 02/863446
Gin Rosa - Donini -
P.za San Babila, 4/b
☎ 02/76000461
I Giardini di Marzo - P.za Santo Stefano
☎ 02/58303776
Il Sole - Via Curtatone,5
☎ 02/55188500
Illi Bar - P.za F.Meda, 3
☎ 02/76021024
Jamaica - Via Brera, 32
☎ 02/876723
La Loggia - Via Larga, 8
☎ 02/86460731
Le Piramidi - P.za XXIV Maggio, 7
☎ 02/58101620
Le Trottoir - C.so Garibaldi, 1
☎ 02/801002

Magenta - Via Carducci,13
☎ 02/8053808
Marchesi - Via Santa Maria alla Porta, 11/a
☎ 02/876730
Portnoy - Via De Amicis, 1
☎ 02/58113429
Quadronno - Via Quadronno, 34
ang. C.so di P.ta Vigentina ☎ 02/58306612
Sant'Ambroeus - C.so Matteotti, 7
☎ 02/76000540
Stradone di S. Teresa
Via della Moscova , 29 ☎ 02/6597862
Taveggia
Via Visconti di Modrone, 2
☎ 02/76021257
Up To You - Via Vetere, 9
☎ 02/8323376
Victoria - Via Clerici, 1
☎ 02/8690834

Pubs and Pianobars

Babuscka - Via Imbonati, 12
☎ 0338/8741858
Black Friars - Corso Porta Ticinese, 16
☎ 02/58106130
Edi's Pub - Via Mantova, 10
☎ 02/55184192
Gambrinus - Viale Teodorico, 7
☎ 02/3319951
Green House Pub - Via Gallarate, 113
☎ 02/3085635
Irish Pub Mulligans - Via Govone, 28
☎ 02/3451694
Live Music Grillo Parlante
Alzaia Naviglio Grande, 36
☎ 02/89409321
Palo Alto Café - Corso Porta Romana, 106
☎ 02/58314071
Pink Floyd - Via S. Teodosio, 37
☎ 02/2363460
Sayonara American Piano Bar
Via Ippolito Nievo, 1 ☎ 02/436635
The Beer Garden - Viale Pasubio, 14
☎ 02/6597370
Vascello La Stiva - Piazza Greco
☎ 02/6704353

Live theatres and Movie theatres

Teatro alla Scala - Via Filodrammatici, 2
☎ 02/88791
Teatro delle Erbe - Via Mercato, 3
☎ 02/876907
Teatro Nazionale - Piazza Piemonte, 12
☎ 02/48006415
Piccolo Teatro Città di Milano
Via Rivoli, 6 ☎ 02/88462236
Ambasciatori - Corso Vittorio Emanuele II, 30
☎ 02/77003306
Anteo Spazio Cinema - Via Milazzo, 9
☎ 02/65997732
Arcobaleno - Via Tunisia, 11
☎ 02/29406054
Ariston - G. del Corso, 1 ☎ 02/76023806
Arlecchino - Via San Pietro all'Orto, 9
☎ 02/76001214
Brera Multisala - Corso Garibaldi, 99
☎ 02/29001890
Cavour - Piazza Cavour, 3
☎ 02/6595779
Centrale - Via Torino, 30
☎ 02/874826
Corallo - Largo Corsia dei Servi
☎ 02/76020721
Corso - G. del Corso
☎ 02/76002184
Ducale - Piazza Napoli, 27
☎ 02/47719279
Eliseo - Via Torino, 64
☎ 02/8692752

Maestoso - Corso Lodi, 39
☎ 02/5516438
Manzoni - Via Manzoni, 40
☎ 02/76020650
Mediolanum - G. Vittorio Emanuele II, 24
☎ 02/76020818
Mignon - G. del Corso, 4
☎ 02/76022343
Multisala Colosseo - Via Monte Nero, 84
☎ 02/59901361
Nuovo Arti - Via Mascagni, 8
☎ 02/76020048
Pasquirolo
Corso Vittorio Emanuele II, 38
☎ 02/76020757
Plinius - Viale Abruzzi, 28
☎ 02/29531103
President - Largo Augusto, 1
☎ 02/76022190
Splendor - Via Donatello, 37
☎ 02/2365124

DISCOTHEQUES

Acid - Via Copernico, 17
☎ 02/66980880
Al Vascello - Piazza Greco
☎ 02/66714934
American Disaster - Via Boscovich, 48
☎ 02/29531728
Beau Geste - Piazza Velasca, 4
☎ 02/8900692
Conir - Vicolo Fiori, 2
☎ 02/876016
Cosmo - Via Ricciarelli, 11
☎ 02/40091894
Curufin - Piazza Velasca, 4
☎ 02/86462017
Disco 3 In - Via Paolo Sarpi, 15
☎ 02/341803
Discoteque Show Club
Via Varanini, 2
☎ 02/2841092

Ebony Note - Via F. Bocconi
☎ 02/58301651
Felix - Via Gonzaga, 5
☎ 02/8692107
Gls - Via Costanza, 3
☎ 02/4816312
HD - Via Tajani, 11
☎ 02/718990
Hollywood - Corso Como, 15
☎ 02/6598996
Il Sottomarino Giallo - V.le Abruzzi, 48
☎ 02/29401047
La Nuova Idea - Via De Castillia, 30
☎ 02/69007859
Magic Rock Cafè - Via Sant'Antonio, 4
☎ 02/58309182
Magica - Piazza Castello, 1
☎ 02/860307
Nepentha - Piazza Diaz, 1
☎ 02/804837
New Parco delle Rose
Via Fabio Massimo, 36 ☎ 02/55212526
Perla lu - Viale Monte Grappa, 14
☎ 02/6597824
Pink Elephant - Via Sarpi, 33
☎ 02/3311290
Propaganda - Via Castelbarco, 11
☎ 02/58310682
Rolling Stone
Corso XXII Marzo, 32
☎ 02/733172
Rosis - Gall. San Babila, 4/c
☎ 02/782429
Tecla Time - Via Santa Tecla, 3
☎ 02/86464205
Time - Corso Lodi, 65
☎ 02/5397347
Tucano - Via Assunta, 8
☎ 02/531420
Tulipano Nero
Viale San Michele del Carso, 20
☎ 02/48016376
23 RD Street - Via Cesariano, 10
☎ 02/33101906

MUSEUMS

Leonardo's Last Supper
Piazza Santa Maria delle Grazie, 2
☎ 02/4987588 (for information on the hours)

Modern Art Gallery
Via Palestro, 16
☎ 02/76002819
Tuesday - Sunday: 9,30-17,30

Archeological Museum
Corso Magenta, 15 ☎ 02/86450011
Tuesday - Sunday: 9,30-17,30

Art Museum Marinara "Ugo Mursia"
Via Sant'Andrea, 6 ☎ 02/783797

Museums of the Castello Sforzesco
Piazza Castello ☎ 02/62083940
Every day: 9-17,40

Museum of the Basilica di S. Ambrogio
Piazza S. Ambrogio, 15 ☎ 02/86450895
Wednesday - Monday: 10-12;15-17
Saturday and holidays: 15-17

Cathedral Museum
Piazza Duomo, 14 ☎ 02/860358
Tuesday - Sunday: 9,30-13,30; 15-18
(open Monday on holidays).

Leonardo da Vinci Museum of Science and Technoloy
Via S. Vittore, 21 ☎ 02/485551
Tuesday - Friday: 9,30-16,50
Saturday and Sunday: 9,30-18,20
(open Monday on holidays).

Museum of Milan - Via Sant'Andrea, 6
☎ 02/783797
Tuesday - Sunday: 9-13; 14-18

Natural History Museum
Corso Venezia, 55 ☎ 02/781312
Monday - Friday: 9-18
Saturday and holidays: 9,30-18,30

Manzoni Museum - Via G. Morone, 1
☎ 02/86460403
Monday - Friday: 9,30-12; 14-16

Naval Museum
Via S. Vittore, 21 ☎ 02/4817270
Tuesday - Friday: 9,30-17

Poldi Pezzoli Museum - Via Manzoni,12
☎ 02/794889
Tuesday - Sunday: 10-19

La Scala Theater Museum
Piazza della Scala, 2 ☎ 02/8879473
Tuesday - Sunday: 9-10; 14-17

Pavilion of Contemporary Art
Via Palestro, 14 ☎ 02/62086537
Tuesday - Sunday: 9,30-18,30

Ambrosian Picture Gallery
Piazza Pio XI, 2 - ☎ 02/806921
Tuesday - Sunday: 10-17,30

Brera Picture Gallery - Via Brera, 28
☎ 02/722631
Tuesday - Saturday: 9-17

INDEX OF THE ITINERARIES

FIRST ITINERARY Page 7
- The Cathedral Plaza " 8
- The Cathedral " 10
- The Royal Palace " 28
- The Cathedral Museum " 29
- Church of San Gottardo in Corte " 32
- The Victor Emmanuel II Arcade " 33
- Piazza della Scala " 34
- La Scala Theater " 37
- Church of San Fedele " 39
- Poldi-Pezzoli Museum " 38
- Basilica of San Babila " 43

SECOND ITINERARY Page 47
- Castello Sforzesco " 48
- Sempione Park " 67
- Arco della Pace (Arch of Peace) " 68

THIRD ITINERARY Page 69
- The Brera Palace " 70
- The Brera Art Gallery " 71
- Church of San Marco " 82
- Royal Villa " 84
- Gallery of Modern Art " 84

FOURTH ITINERARY Page 89
- The Church of San Maurizio or Great Monastery " 90
- Basilica of Saint Ambrose " 92
- Museum of the Basilica of St. Ambrose " 97
- The Postern of Saint Ambrose " 98
- The L. da Vinci National Museum of Science and Technology " 99
- Church of Santa Maria delle Grazie " 101
- Leonardo's Last Supper " 105
- Ambrosian Picture Gallery " 113

FIFTH ITINERARY Page 117
- Church of Sant'Eustorgio " 118
- Basilica of S. Lorenzo Maggiore " 127
- Church of Santa Maria della Passione " 130
- Church of Santa Maria at San Satiro " 131
- Church of Santa Maria at San Celso " 132
- Church of S. Carlo al Corso " 134
- The Lazzeretto " 135
- Church of S. Nazaro Maggiore " 135
- Church of San Simpliciano 137
- The Naviglio Canal " 138
- The Main Hospital Ca' Granda " 139

INDEX

- Ambrosian Library Page 116
- Arches of Porta Nuova " 42
- Arco della Pace (Arch of Peace) " 68

- Broletto Nuovo " 45
- Broletto Vecchio " 28

- Casa degli Omenoni " 38
- Castello Sforzesco " 48

CHURCHES
- Cathedral " 10
- Saint Ambrose " 92
- San Babila " 43
- San Carlo al Corso " 134
- Sant'Eustorgio " 118
- San Fedele " 37
- San Francesco da Paola " 42
- San Giuseppe " 70
- San Gottardo in Corte " 32
- San Lorenzo Maggiore " 127
- San Marco " 82
- Santa Maria delle Grazie " 101
- Santa Maria della Passione " 130
- Santa Maria at San Celso " 132
- Santa Maria at San Satiro " 131
- San Maurizio (or Great Monastery) " 90
- San Nazaro Maggiore " 135
- San Simpliciano " 137
- San Vittore al Corpo " 98

Column of the Lion " 43

Welcome to Milan!

Milan was founded by the Insubres, a Celtic people of Northern Italy, around 400 B.C. Starting about 225 B.C. the Insubres were constantly at war with the Romans who succeeded in conquering the city in 222, after which it became known as "Mediolanum", which means "in the middle of the plain". Its inhabitants made an alliance with Hannibal and rebelled against the Romans but were reduced to obedience in 196 B.C. and compelled to pay allegiance to Rome. Benefiting from the laws enacted by the capital of the Empire, it soon prospered and became the main industrial and commercial center of Northern Italy.

Between the end of the 1st and the beginning of the 2nd century, Milan was converted to Christianity and a century later the first Diocese was founded. Throughout this period the bishops had an increasingly important role in the life of the city, especially during the time of St. Ambrose (4th century). It was the seat of the Western Emperors until the time of Theodosius, but when Honorius became emperor in 404, he moved his capital to Ravenna. During the period of the barbarian invasions, Milan was attacked by the Burgundians and in 539 was destroyed by the Goths under Vitigis.

From 568 to 774, under the domination of the Lombards, Milan lost much of its former importance because the Lombards decided to establish their capital in Pavia. When the Franks had conquered the Lombards, the situation improved slightly because of the intense political activity of the Milanese bishops. By the middle of the 10th century, the clergy and the wealthy classes had gained political supremacy and were able to establish order in the city so that commerce could flourish once again.

The religious conflicts and the political and social strife which occurred between 1018 and

Victor Emmanuel II and Napoleon III enter Milan (Museum of the Risorgimento)

Duca d'Aosta Plaza with the Pirelli skyscraper and the main railway station

1045 caused the Milanese to side first with one, then with the other, foreign emperor trying to gain supremacy in Italy, until the age of the free communes. During the second half of the 11th century and the first half of the 12th, Milan was involved in the long power struggle between the Empire and the Papacy. This situation continued until the creation of the statutes founding the free communes, which then developed very rapidly and enabled Milan to recover from the devastating consequences of the policy of the Emperor Frederick, who destroyed the city in 1162. In fact, within a few years, Milan had formed an alliance with other Northern Italian cities called the Lombard League, whose troops met and defeated the Emperor at the battle of Legnano.

A period of relative peace followed, during which the city prospered, despite continual internecine strife, until the second half of the 13th century when a form of local despotism called the "signoria" (seignory) arose, as powerful families fought for supremacy within the city. Eventually the Visconti family prevailed and ruled despotically as the lords or "Signori" of Milan from 1330 to 1447. They did, however, have the merit of producing a period of economic, artistic and cultural prosperity. After the end of the domination of the Viscontis came the short-lived Ambrosian Republic, followed by the signoria of the Sforza family who ruled over Milan from 1450 to 1535.
During this period the history of Milan is inextricably bound to the history of the political activities of the Visconti and Sforza families and was subject to all their vicissitudes, as they strug-

The Cathedral Plaza in a reproduction by Giuseppe Migliara

gled to maintain power within the city and allied themselves with Charles VIII of France and other powerful rulers who were continually tempted to invade the Italian peninsula. In 1535 the struggle between Francis I of France and Charles V of Spain was resolved in favor of the latter and from 1535 until 1706 Milan reluctantly came under Spanish domination.
From 1706, following the Wars of Succession, in accordance with the agreements reached by the contracting parties, Milan fell under Austrian domination which lasted, apart from a brief interlude, until the Napoleonic era, when the Cisalpine Republic was established in 1797. However, the industrial and cultural enterprise for which Milan was to become famous prospered under Austrian rule. During the Napoleonic period the city became the capital, first of the Italian Republic and then of the Kingdom of Italy in 1805, but the rapid decline of Napoleon's fortunes gave Austria the opportunity to occupy Lombardy again in 1845, so that Milan remained under Austrian rule until 1859.
Although the Milanese were oppressed by the Austrian rule, they were not indifferent to the cause of the unification of Italy, and became an example to all the Italian people for the courage they showed in confronting the Austrian army during the epic battle known as the "Five Days" (March 18th-23rd, 1848). Although this insurrection was put down due to the overwhelming numbers of their adversary, and it could not be turned to immediate advantage by the promoters of Italian independence, it succeeded in rallying the Italian people to the cause and was one of the historic events that eventually led to the unification of Italy.
The history of Milan, as an independent political entity, ends in 1859 when the city became part of the newly born Italian nation with all the weight of its political, religious and cultural history, its commercial and industrial enterprise behind it, constituting a vital and important part of the new state. In fact, the Milanese have always maintained that Milan is, from a moral standpoint, the true capital of Italy.

First Itinerary

1 The Cathedral Plaza
2 The Cathedral
3 The Royal Palace (with the Cathedral Museum)
4 Church of San Gottardo in Corte
5 The Victor Emmanuel II Arcade (La Galleria)
6 Piazza della Scala
7 La Scala Theatre
8 Church of San Fedele
9 Poldi-Pezzoli Museum

The Cathedral Plaza
Piazza del Duomo

This magnificent square is said to be the mirror of Milan and the Milanese. In fact its citizens pour in and out of it at every hour of the day; whether it is ablaze with sunlight or full of snow, they pass in a hurry and seem almost unaware of its beauty, its gleaming space, its imposing, white cathedral. This is not true however, since the speed at which a Milanese thinks is the same as his rhythm of work and when he passes by he only needs a glance at it to be comforted and excited, and have his heart fill with pride before disappearing into the darkness of the subway or being swallowed up in the traffic.

The vast rectangular plaza as it appears today, was designed in 1865 by the architect Giuseppe Mengoni. In the center stands the **Monument to Victor Emmanuel II** which is by Ercole Rosa (1896). This equestrian statue in bronze represents the *King at the battle of San Martino*, while the base shows the *Entry of the Piedmontese and French troops into Milan after the Battle of Magenta* (1859). The immense bulk of the cathedral forms a background to the square and is flanked on the left, by the *Palazzo Settentrionale* (the Northern Palace) with porticos which open into the *Victor Emmanuel Arcade* (Galleria Vittorio Emanuele) and to the right, by the *Palazzo Meridionale* (the Southern Palace) also with porticos, after which there are two buildings with loggias; at the other end, the square is completed by the *Palazzo dell'Orologio* (the Palace of the Clock). The two main subway lines, called the red and the yellow line, intersect at the station beneath this square.

The Cathedral Plaza

Monument to Victor Emmanuel II by Ercole Rosa

Aerial view of the Cathedral Plaza

The Cathedral

The Cathedral
Il Duomo

The cathedral is the largest monument in Milan and the most gigantic and complex Gothic building in Italy. Building of this colossal structure was started in 1386 and required centuries of work and the contributions of many generations. It was begun at the wish of the Milanese people encouraged by their archbishop, Antonio da Saluzzo, and under the patronage of the Duke Gian Galeazzo Visconti. The foundations were built over the pre-existing 9th century church of Santa Maria Maggiore. The name of the first architect is not known but he was certainly inspired by French Gothic cathedrals. Scholars have attributed the original design to various architects, including Simone da Orsenigo who was the first construction engineer to work on it, Marco Frisone da Campione, Giovannino de' Grassi and others. Over the centuries, however, various Italian, French and German artists participated in the design and construction, and this is the reason for the enormous variety of different styles in the building, which are nonetheless, harmoniously blended. In 1389 a Parisian, Nicolao De Bonaventuris took part in the work, and to him we owe the design of the great apse windows. Later, Giovannino and Salomone de' Grassi directed construction as did Gabriele Stornaloco from Piacenza, the Germans Johann of Freiburg, Heinrich of Gmünden, Ulrich of Füssyngen, the Fleming Corrado Bruges and Jean Mignot of Paris, after whom foreign architects no longer participated in the project. In 1400 Filippino degli Organi was appointed master of the works and designed the fretwork of the apse, as well as that of the vaults, of the terraces and of the capitals. From then onwards, work on the colossal structure went ahead quickly, so much so that in

The Cathedral: close-up view of the South side

Apse of the Cathedral

1418, Pope Martin V, who was passing through Milan, was able to consecrate the high altar. In the second half of the 15th century, by decree of the Duke Francesco Sforza, the supervision of the work was entrusted to the Solaris and to the great Giovanni Antonio Amadeo who designed the drum of the cupola. After the death of Amadeo (1522) work came to a temporary standstill, until 1567 when the archbishop Carlo Borromeo ordered construction to be continued under the direction of Pellegrino Tibaldi

Façade of the Cathedral with its great doors

(called "Il Pellegrini") who designed the façade in classical Baroque style. In 1572 Archbishop Borromeo consecrated the Cathedral once again. After Pellegrini, Martino Bassi and Lelio Buzzi worked on the Cathedral, and then, in the 17th century, Francesco Maria Richini first, and later, Carlo Buzzi who began the construction of the façade designed by Pellegrini but made modifications to give it a more Gothic appearance. In 1765, the tallest spire was raised, and, in 1774, the gilded statue of the Virgin called the

Statues on the façade of the Cathedral: Apostles and Prophets

"*Madonnina*" was added. In 1805, Napoleon entrusted Carlo Amati with the task of finishing the work on the façade. The construction of the spires and the staircase turrets around the drum continued throughout the 19th century. The doors of the façade, except for the central Pogliaghi door

(1908) were placed in position from 1948 to 1965. Over the centuries major maintenance work has also been done on the Cathedral, especially during the 1980s and 1990s.

Dimensions and characteristics of the building - For the amount of surface area covered, the Cathedral of Milan (14,000 sq. yd.) is the second largest church in Italy and the third

Main door of the Cathedral

The Cathedral: one of the panels on the central door

largest in the world, surpassed only by St. Peter's in Rome and by the Cathedral of Seville in Spain. The outside is 510 ft. long and 214 ft. wide; the transept is 299 ft. wide. The façade is 182 ft. high and 221 ft. wide. There are 135 spires and the tallest, with the gold "*Madonnina*" is 356 ft. high. The facings are of Candoglia marble which is pinky white with bluish veining. There are 2,245 statues on the outside of the cathedral; if one includes the ones inside, the figure comes to 3,159 (excluding those in the embrasures of the windows). There are 96 gigantic gargoyles.

The façade - The lower part, up to

The Cathedral: one of the panels on the central door

the first series of windows is Baroque and was executed in the 16th century according to designs by Pellegrini. The upper part, executed in the following centuries, returned to the Gothic style. Six immense pillars surmounted by spires separate the five great 16th century doors and two rows of windows crowned by balconies which, as they go upwards, join together towards the center to form the cusp. The supports on which the pillars rest are decorated with reliefs representing *Stories from the Bible*, which were carved in the 17th and 18th centuries, and the bases of the pillars themselves are decorated with *telamons* (male figures used as supporting

The Cathedral: central nave

columns) of the same epoch. The upper series of statues, supported by consoles, represent *Apostles and Prophets* and were sculpted at the beginning of the 19th century. The friezes of the first doorway on the left are by Giovan Battista Crespi, while the bronze door with panels representing the *Edict of Constantine,* is by Arrigo Minerbi (1948): the decoration of the second door is also by Crespi and the bronze door with panels representing *Episodes from the Life of St. Ambrose* is by Giannino Castiglioni (1950); the magnificent doorway of the central entrance, surrounded by a sumptuous frame of flowers and animals, was based upon designs by Francesco M. Richini; while the beautiful door in bronze with decorations representing *Episodes from the Life of Mary* is by Lodovico Pogliaghi (1894-1908); the frieze of the

fourth doorway is by Crespi and the bronze door with panels representing the *History of Milan from the Destruction by Barbarossa to the Victory of Legnano* is by Franco Lombardi but was completed by Virgilio Pessina (1950): the frieze of the fifth doorway is by Carlo Biffi, and the door in bronze representing the *Important Episodes in the History of the Cathedral,* is by Luciano Menguzzi (1965).

Interior - The overwhelming proportions of the cathedral and the evocative mystical atmosphere created by the soft light that filters through the multicolored stained - glass windows inspire the visitor to turn his thoughts to the Creator of all things. The cathedral is supported by 52 immense pillars, the nave is divided into 5 aisles and the transept into 3 aisles. The capitals of the pillars are adorned with foliate decoration while the tops of the pillars of the central nave are surrounded by a ring of niches containing statues of *Saints.* Around the deep apse runs a vast ambulatory. The recently restored floor was based on a design by Pellegrini. The central nave which leads to the drum and the central nave of the transept are exactly twice as wide as the side aisles. The great central doorway of the internal façade is by Fabio Mangone and is surmounted by statues of *St. Ambrose* and *St. Charles* by Pompeo Marchesi and Gaetano Monti respectively.

The Right Aisle - First span, 11th century *Tomb of the Archbishop Ariberto da Intimiano,* inventor of the Carroccio. Above the tomb there is a reproduction of an 11th century Lombard copper *Crucifix* of great interest (the original is in the Cathedral Museum). To the left, a stone plaque with an inscription commemorating the foundation of the Cathedral in the year 1386. - Second span, the *Mausoleum of the Archbishop Ottone Visconti* (died 1295) in

Funeral monument to Gian Giacomo de' Medici by Leone Leoni (right transept)

red marble (14th century). Fourth span, the *Sarcophagus of Marco Carelli* by Filippino degli Organi (1406). - Fifth span, plaque with the plan for the façade of the cathedral presented by G. Brentano in 1886; on the left, *Monument to Cardinal Vimercati* by Bambaia. The 26 panes of the large windows, with *Stories from the New Testament* are only a part of a great window which was reconstructed by Bertini. - Sixth span, altar by Pellegrini with an altarpiece representing the *Visit of St. Peter to St. Agatha* by F. Zuccari (1597) - Seventh span, altar by Pellegrini. - Eighth span, altar by Pellegrini with a marble altarpiece with a *Sacred Conversation* of 1393. The transept starts here and from its center rises the lofty drum.

The Right Transept - On the far right nave of the right transept, *Monument to Gian Giacomo de' Medici,* known as the "*Medeghino*" (d. 1555) marquis of Marignano, and a general of Charles V: a masterpiece by Leone Leoni (1560-63). The monument is decorated with bas-reliefs and a bronze statue of the deceased dressed in Roman armor in the central shrine. The statue to the left, represents *Militia*, and the bas-relief above it, the *Adda*; to the right, the statue of *Peace*, and above, the bas-relief representing the *Ticino*. The statues on the external columns represent *Prudence* and *Fame*. On the walls at the end of the nave we find a small 16th century altar in precious marble, decorated with two copper statues donated by Pope Pius IV. The large window with *Stories of St. James the Greater* is by Corrado de Mochis 1554-1564.

In the apse of the central aisle of the transept, there is the *Chapel of St. Giovanni Bono,* Bishop of Milan (17th century); the three windows show *Episodes from the Life of the Saint*, by Giovanni Bertini.

In the left aisle of the right arm of the transept, between two little doors, we find the underground passage to the Archbishop's Palace, and over it, a stupendous stained glass window representing *Scenes from the Life of Saint Catherine of Alexandria*, by Biagio and Giuseppe Arcimboldi (1556). The next altar has a marble altarpiece with the *Presentation of Mary at the Temple* by Bambaia (1543). In the stained glass window, *Story of St. Martin*; further ahead, on a pedestal, the gruesome statue of *St. Bartholomew Flayed Alive* by Marco d'Agrate (1562), which is very famous but is actually of little artistic value. On the following altar a marble altar piece with the *Martyrdom of St. Agnes* by C. Beretta and a statue of *St. Ambrose.*

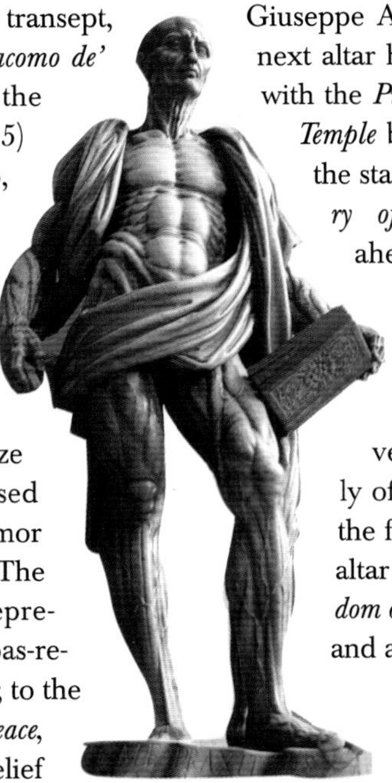

St. Bartholomew Flayed Alive by Marco d'Agrate (right transept)

The Drum - To get to the presbytery one crosses the magnificent octago-

nal drum (221 ft. high), which rises above four great pointed arches. On the pinnacles of the arches there are busts of the *Doctors of the Church* by Cristoforo Solari; the statues of Prophets and Sybils placed on lintels along the ring of internal arches (60 in all) are of the 15th century. On the floor at the joining of the arms of the cross there is a bronze railing which encloses the "Scurolo" or Vault of San Carlo located beneath.

The Presbytery - Ten pillars restored in the 1980s and linked to each other by a marble enclosure surround the presbytery which Pellegrini raised to make space for the crypt. With their backs to the pillars at the entrance, stand two pulpits in embossed bronze and copper with the *Symbols of the Evangelists* (left), and the *Doctors of the Church* (right); on both parapets *Stories from the Old and New Testaments* (16th - 17th centuries). In the first part of the presbytery, which is occupied by the senatorial *Choir*, there are two colossal organs of the 16th century, one on each side. Further ahead, is the staircase leading to the *Sanctuary* containing the Great Altar: lavish decoration covers the original altar consecrated by Martin V in 1418. Above stands the great ciborium in gilded bronze flanked by two *Angels* as candle holders supported by eight little columns, beautifully executed by Andrea Pellizzone (1581-90), designed by Pellegrini. It encloses the Tabernacle, supported by four *Angels* and decorated with reliefs representing *Episodes from the Life of Jesus* and crowned by small statues of *Christ* and the *Apostles* by the Solaris (1561). The whole sanctuary is surrounded by a magnificent 3 level choir stall in walnut, carved between 1572 and 1620, based on a design by Pellegrini. In the vault towards the altar there is a copper grate with *God the Father*, by Jacopino da Tradate and under it lies the *Holy Nail* which, according to tradition, was given to Constantine by St. Helen and was then found by St. Ambrose at a blacksmith's.

Crypt - Two doors in the façade of the sacristy behind the choir-stalls lead to the crypt which was designed by Pellegrini. The stucco carvings which decorate the vaults were added in the 16th century. From here, going down a few steps, one reaches the underground chapel called the **Scurolo di San Carlo** (Vault of St. Charles). The octagonal shaped vault was built according to the designs of Richini (1606). It is lavishly decorated in silver leaf with eight bas-reliefs on the ceiling representing the *Deeds of the Saint*, executed by artists of the 17th century. The body of San Carlo, in papal vestments decorated with gems, is enclosed in a sumptuous urn of rock crystal which was donated by Philip IV of Spain. The stairway next to the door of the sacristy leads to the *Cathedral Treasure* where tapestries and precious works of art in gold and ivory are preserved.

The Ambulatory - The Ambulatory surrounds the presbytery from which it is separated by a handsome marble enclosure designed by Pellegrini. Along the upper part runs an attic

The Cathedral: door leading to the Southern sacristy by Hans von Fernach (around 1393)

with panels, separated by statues, with 17th century bas-reliefs representing *Stories from the Life of Mary*. Next comes the stupendously ornate *Portal of the southern sacristy*, by the German Hans von Fernach assisted by Porrino and Giovannino de' Grassi. Inside the sacristy, above the entrance, we find the *Martyrdom of St. Thecla* by Aurelio Luini (1592). The basin to the right with a medallion in the cusp with *Jesus and the Samaritan Woman,* is by Giovannino de' Grassi (1396). To the left, in the niche, *Christ at the Pillar* by Cristoforo Solari. The enormous 17th century walnut cupboards, which cover the lower part of the walls, contain the precious objects which form part of the Treasure, including the famous painted processional panel with the *Madonna of the Idea*, bearing the forged signature of Michelino da Besozzo. Beyond the sacristy door in the second span are the remains of a 15th century fresco with *the Madonna Suckling the Child*, known as the *Virgin of Help*; above this, on a large Gothic

The Cathedral, Crypt of San Carlo

The Cathedral: multi-colored stained glass window seen from the inside

The Cathedral: view of the terraces, the drum and spires

corbel, the beautiful statue of *Martin V*, by Jacopino da Tradate (1424). The plaque below covers the remains of the *condottieri*, Nicolò and Francesco Piccinino. Next comes the *Monument to Cardinal Marino Caracciolo* (d. 1538) by Bambaia. Third span, framed marble slab known as "Chrismon Sancti Ambrosii", and bas-relief of 1389 by a German artist, with a *Pietà* and two *Angels*. Fourth span, *commemorative plaque* of the consecration of the church, by the archbishop Carlo Borromeo, September 20th, 1577. The three stained glass windows of the apse contain *Stories from the New Testament, Stories from the Apocalypse*, and *Stories from the Old Testament*. Flanking the great windows we find statues of the 14th and 15th century. Fifth span, a 3rd century *Crucifix* dressed in liturgical vestments, under glass. Sixth span: *Statue of Pius IV giving his Benediction* by Angelo Marini (1567). The frescoes representing the *Crucifix between the Virgin and Saints* and *the Madonna with Child and St. John the Baptist* are both from the beginning of the 15thcentury. Seventh span: the marvelous *Portal of the northern sacristy*, by Giacomo da Campione (14th century); the cusp above the portal contains a relief of the *Redeemer Giving his Benediction*. Inside, we can admire the vault frescoed with *Angels* by Camillo Procaccini (1611). The floor is by Marco da Carona (beginning of the 15th century) and in the niche is a statue of particular interest, the *Redeemer* by Antonio da Viggiù.

The Left Transept - Along the right aisle we find two altars with marble altar pieces with *St. Thecla among the Lions* by Carlo Beretta (1754) and the *Crucifix and Saints* by Marcantonio Prestinari (1605). The beautiful stained glass window shows the *Stories of St. John of Damascus* by Nicolò da Varallo (15th century). The small door

Close-up view of the terraces, the drum and the spires of the Cathedral

in the wall beyond leads to *the "Stairway of the Princes"* which goes up to the terraces; in the past it was reserved exclusively for important personages. In the small apse of the middle nave, one finds the chapel of the *Madonna of the Tree*, designed by Richini in Baroque

Trivulzio candlestick attributed to the French goldsmith Nicolas of Verdun (left transept)

style; on the altar *Madonna and Child* by Elia Vincenzo Buzzi (1768). In the central aisle, in front of the altar, the celebrated seven-arm bronze *Trivulzio Candlestick* which is over 16 ft. high, by a 13th century French artist. The famous candlestick was donated by a member of the Trivulzio family in 1562. In the left aisle, the altar with 15th and 16th century statues including *St. Jerome* and *St. Augustine* by Cristoforo Solari.

The Left aisle - The eighth span: altar by Pellegrini, with a canvas by Barocci (1603). The seventh span: above the altar is the *Betrothal of the Virgin* by Enea Salmeggia (1600) between two statues of *Prophets* by Samaini. The sixth span: above the altar a wooden *Crucifix* which was carried by San Carlo in procession during the plague of 1576. The fifth span: *Monument to Alessio Tarchetta*, captain at the time of Francesco Sforza, completely remade in 1832; fragments of the original by Amadeo are to be found in the Museum of the Castello Sforzesco. The fourth span: window designed by Pellegrini with *Stories of the Four Crowned Saints* and executed by Corrado de Mochis (1568). The third span: *Monument of the Three Arcimboldi Archbishops,* attributed to Alessi. The second span: two red Verona marble slabs with reliefs representing eight of the *Apostles*, from the end of the 12th century. To the left, between the columns, the canopied *Baptistery*, designed by Pellegrini; the font is an ancient Roman porphyry urn. In the first span, against the wall under the window, there is a sundial with the

symbol of *Capricorn* (1786). A narrow stairway at the inside of the façade leads down to the Paleochristian archaeological excavations, about 13 ft. below the present level of the Piazza.

Climb to the Terraces - Once one has visited the cathedral both inside and outside and seen the view of the right side and the façade from the little plaza called Piazzetta Reale, a visit to the terraces is indispensable. The terraces can be reached through the two entrances located at the far end of the sides of the cathedral where there is a climb up 158 steps. An elevator is provided, however, at the corner of the transepts towards the apse on the outside of the cathedral. The feeling experienced by the visitor is unforgettable, unique, entirely different from the sensations given by Giotto's Campanile in Florence, or the dome of St. Peter's in the Vatican, or even the tower of the Town Hall in Siena from all of which one can enjoy stupendous views of the respective cities and the surrounding hills. From the terraces of Milan cathedral one not only grasps the vast size and beauty of this monument, but the mere contact with the great blocks of marble, the forest of spires of every size, the numerous statues, the gigantic gargoyles, is absolutely fascinating. The visitor may also admire the magnificent *drum* from here; it is Amadeo's masterpiece (1490) and is surmounted by the tallest spire crowned with the famous statue of the *Madonnina* in gilded bronze, which is over 13 ft. tall and was created by the goldsmith Bini in 1774 based on a model by G. Perego.

The Cathedral: statue of the Madonnina on the highest spire, by Giuseppe Bini (1774)

The Royal Palace (with the Cathedral Museum)

The Royal Palace
Palazzo Reale

The palace stands in the rectangular square on the southern side of the cathedral; it is a wide building with a Neoclassical front and two lateral wings. It is of ancient origin and during its long history has undergone many changes. In the 12th century, the **Broletto Vecchio**, which was where the Consuls who governed the Free Commune had their headquarters, was built on this site. In 1310, the Viscontis established themselves there, and in 1330 Azzone transformed the palace into a sumptuous residence, making it the Ducal court of the Viscontis. In 1385 the Viscontis went to live in the Castle when the front of the palace was demolished to make room for the Cathedral. In the 16th and 17th centuries the building was radically restructured and became the seat of the Spanish governors; in addition, it was the site of the first Milanese opera house. In 1771-78, when the Milanese state was under Austrian domination, the archduke Ferdinand ordered the architect Giuseppe Piermarini to modify the building once more, destroying the façade

A room of the Cathedral Museum

and rearranging the great rooms, according to the needs of the times. With the Unification of Italy, it became the Royal Palace and later, a Museum with objects from the Milanese Neoclassical period. The building was destroyed by bombing during the war (1943) and almost all of the collections were lost. It now houses the **Civico Museo d'Arte Contemporanea** (Municipal Museum of Contemporary Art) which was founded in the 1980s and its collections include works by Modigliani, De Chirico, Sironi, Carrà, De Pisis, Morandi and Rosai.

Cathedral Museum, statue of Gian Galeazzo Visconti dressed as St. George by Giorgio Solari (Room II)

The Cathedral Museum
Museo del Duomo

The Museum occupies a number of ground floor rooms of the Royal Palace and provides a fascinating overall view of how the Cathedral developed through the centuries. The collection represents an extraordinary record of the history of sculpture and decorative arts in Northern Italy and shows how the Cathedral was the inspiring and stimulating focus for almost all artistic endeavor in Lombardy from the 14th century on.

Room I - Great Copper-gilt embossed effigy of the *Heavenly Father* by Beltramino da Rho (1416).

Room II (or *Room of the Origins*) - In the center: Statue of *Gian Galeazzo Visconti as St. George* by Giorgio Solari (1404). On the walls, three marble statues (*Two Angels* and *a Prophet*) formerly on the Carelli spire - Burgundian School, end of the 15th century. *Head of the Redeemer* and *St. Agnes* by Briosco. *Madonna and Child,* a painted wooden statue by Bernardo da Venezia.

Room III (or *Visconti Room*) - Once the stables of the Royal Palace. The ground plan is rectangular and contains several Visconti-era objects by Rhenish-Bohemian and Lombard craftsmen, including *St. Peter the Apostle, St. John the Evangelist* and the plaster cast of the *Monument to Pope Martin V* made for the Cathedral by Jacopino da Tradate (1421), as well as various *Prophets* and *Saints.*

Room IV (or *Room of the Music Chapel*) - 15th century polyphonic music scores.

Room V (or *Room of the Drum*) - Contains a graphic documentation on the building of the drum and on the works it contains: a remarkable *St. Peter the Apostle,* attributed to Jacobello Dalle Masegne (14th century).

Room VI (or *Room of the Sforza Era*)-

Cathedral Museum, Head of the Redeemer, a 15th century work in gold and copper (Room II)

In the center, a statue of *Galeazzo Maria Sforza* inside a terra cotta apse - a unique example of Lombard sculpture, flanked by *Shield-bearing Warriors*, of the Mantegazza School together with an *Angel bearing a Crown of Thorns*. Various *Sforza shields* on the walls.

Room VII (or *The Embossed Brass Room*) - Remarkable *Crucifix* by Ariberto (1040) in embossed copper and brass; 14th century Rhenish School: *Madonna and Child with two Angels*; and a great *Easter Candlestick* (15th century Lombard School).

Room VIII (or *Sforza Room*) - Pavia and Milanese School sculpture: a remarkable *St. Paul the Hermit* (1470); *St. Lucy and St. Agnes*, attributed to Briosco (1491). Also: Flemish tapestry with *Deposition*.

Room IX (or *Room of the Amadeo Spire*) - Photographic documentation of the *"torrino"* or spire built by Giovanni Antonio Amadeo (1517); the two 16th century statues of *Virtue* and *St. Barbara* and a 16th century Flemish altar - front tapestry with *Scenes of the Passion*.

Room X (or *Room of the Borromeos*) - 17th century art work demonstrating the Counter-Reformation influence of the Borromeos. Carlo and Federico Borromeo (*Altar-front tapestry of San Carlo Borromeo*) and the *Miracle of the Woman in Labor* by Cerano (1610); embossed silver candlestick (1610) and two choir-stalls.

Room XI (or *Tapestry Room*) - On the walls: four tapestry hangings from the series given by the Duke of Mantua to San Carlo Borromeo, showing *Moses receiving the Tablets of*

the Law; the *Crossing of the Red Sea; Moses and the Bronze Serpent;* and *Putti playing.* Also, *Jesus with the Doctors in the Temple,* an early work by Tintoretto and a wooden *Crucifix* of the 17th century Venetian School.

Room XII (or *Room of the Models*) - Various sculptures dating from 1550 to 1700 which represent different sculpture techniques: *St. Helena* and *Madonna* by Marini (1565); *Sacrifice of Elijah* and *Abraham about to Sacrifice Isaac* by Vismara (17th century); *St. Agapitus* and *St. Ambrose* by M. Prestinari (1610) and the *Flight into Egypt* (1624) one of several paintings by Biffi in this room. Wooden and clay models for Mannerist and Baroque statues.

Room XIII (or *Room of the Madonnina*) - Terracotta models of the famous "*Madonnina*" placed on the tallest spire of the Cathedral in 1774 and detail of the *Head* in wood (1771) by Giuseppe Perego, who also modeled the *Warrior Saint* and a terracotta model of *Hercules slaying the Lion of Nemea,* as well as terracotta models by various artists.

Room XIV (or *Room of the 19th century*) - Various examples of restoration and work on the façade, spires and windows. A remarkable *Prophet Beseleel* by Martegani (1867) and *St. Catherine of Alexandria* by Buzzi.

Room XV (or *Gallery of the Graphics*) - A step-by-step illustration of how the Cathedral was built from the beginning to the present day, including the five designs submitted through the centuries for the façade.

Room XVI (or *Room of the Great Model*) - In the middle of the room: a great wooden model of the Cathedral, begun around 1520 with a model of the façade which won the international competition of 1886 submitted by the architect Giuseppe Brentano in 1888. Opposite: another wooden model for the façade presented by Luca Beltrami, carved by Gaetano Moretti also in 1888. Left: wooden model for the façade in Gothic-Baroque style, by Castelli, dated 1656. Right: another design submitted by Galliori in 1786. Also a model of the old bell-tower.

Room XVII (or *Room of the Bronze Doors*) - Sculpture for the five portals of the façade. Of particular interest: *The Sermon on the Mount* (fifteen gilded bronze models) by Francesco Messina (1977).

Room XVIII and XIX (or *Conservation and Restoration Room*) - Interesting documentation concerning the restoration work carried out in order to assure the survival of the ancient structures, using modern technology and equipment.

Room XX (or *Room of the Vestments*) - Access to this room is through Room XII. Its contents are not directly related to other objects in the museum. It contains an important collection of ecclesiastical vestments and liturgical objects from the Cathedral Chapter Sacristy. A remarkable gold and silver *Chasuble* (1805) used during the Coronation of Napoleon, as well as various copes and altar-frontals.

Church of San Gottardo in Corte, the Bell-tower

Church of San Gottardo in Corte

The construction of the church which is incorporated into the Royal Palace (the entrance is from via Pecorari) began in the first half of the 14th century. Azzone Visconti had it built as a chapel for the ducal court, and tradition has it that the Cremonese architect Francesco Pecorari was in charge of the project.

The Gothic character of the outside remains: the portal, the apse with its cusped windows, the upper loggia and the elegant bell-tower by Pecorari. The base of the bell-tower is square: it then becomes octagonal

with slender stone columns covering each of the eight corners; it has monoforus windows on the lower levels and biforus windows on the fourth level, while two layers of superimposed arches adorn the fifth level, above which there is a charming gallery of columns surmounted by a conical cusp with a statue of the *Archangel Gabriel* in copper on the top.

The interior - The interior was completely remodeled and transformed in the Neoclassical period, and contains a fragment of a fresco of the *Crucifixion*, which used to be outside, painted towards the middle of the 14th century by a follower of Giotto; also a canvas by Cerano of *San Carlo in Glory* and the *Sepulcher of Azzone Visconti* by Giovanni di Balduccio.

The Victor Emmanuel II arcade, inside

The Victor Emmanuel II Arcade
Galleria Vittorio Emanuele II

The famous Galleria connects the plaza of the Cathedral to the Piazza della Scala. Building began in 1865 under the direction of Giuseppe Mengoni who died in 1877 after falling from the scaffolding when the Galleria was almost completed. The arcade is known as the "*drawing-room*" of Milan because it is

The Victor Emmanuel II arcade, outside

Piazza della Scala - Monument to Leonardo da Vinci by Pietro Magni

lined with luxurious cafés, elegant shops and important bookshops. It is cross shaped, with one arm 637 feet long and the other 341 feet. The cupola is made of iron and glass and at its highest point is 152 feet tall. The four mosaics in the lunettes above the octagonal court, show *Europe, Africa, Asia* and *America* and in the lunettes at the end of each arm: *Agriculture, Art, Science* and *Industry.*

Piazza della Scala

In the center of the plaza we find the *Monument to Leonardo da Vinci* by Pietro Magni (1872). Four statues of the Milanese disciples of Leonardo, *Marco d'Oggiono, G. Antonio Boltraffio, Andrea Salaino* and *Cesare da Sesto* stand at the corners of the pedestal. In the square is located the La Scala Theater and to the right,

Piazza della Scala, Palazzo Marino

Palazzo Marino, seat of the town council from 1860. This magnificent building which is still one of the most beautiful in Milan, was begun in 1553 under the direction of Galeazzo Alessi, and was commissioned by Tommaso Marino, a Genoese, who died, however, before its completion. The town council finally decided to continue construction and appointed Luca Beltrami (1886-92), who finished the façade which faces the Piazza della Scala and constructed the great internal staircase which leads to the upper stories. The original façade looks onto Piazza S. Fedele. Inside, besides the beautiful portico courtyard with twin columns and loggia, richly decorated with statues and reliefs, there is also an interesting hall called the **Sala dell'Alessi** decorated with gesso reliefs and paintings by Ottavio Semini.

La Scala Theater, inside

La Scala Theater

La Scala is the most famous opera house in the world both because of the superb quality of its performances, and also because it is a testing ground for all the world's singers and musicians. It represents the final goal and highest aspiration of every opera singer. The theater was built in 1778 by Giuseppe Piermarini, where the church of S.

La Scala Theatre in the Plaza of the same name

La Scala Theater Museum, portraits of Giuseppe Verdi, Arturo Toscanini and Giacomo Puccini

Maria dalla Scala used to stand (it was founded in 1381 by Beatrice Regina della Scala the wife of Bernabò Visconti). The outside is rather simple with a Neoclassical façade and is preceded by a small atrium with a portico; a bas-relief of *Apollo's Chariot* (1778) is in the tympanum.

Interior - In the entrance hall there are statues of *Rossini, Bellini, Verdi* and *Donizetti* and a bust of *Stendhal.* The **hall** itself is horseshoe-shaped with four tiers of boxes and two galleries, and is sumptuously decorated in Neoclassic style, faithfully reconstructed after the serious damage suffered during the 1943 bombings. The theater holds 2800 spectators.
In the palace with porticos to the left of La Scala, we find the **Theater Museum** (entrance at no. 2). It contains a valuable collection of objects and relics relating to the history of La Scala Theater and to theater arts from classical antiquity to modern times. The *Verdi collection,* in two rooms, including pictures and drawings relating to Verdi and autographed scores of his compositions, is particularly interesting. The theater library includes the private collections of Renato Simoni and Ruggero Ruggeri. Altogether, it is one of the largest and most complete theatrical collections, with around 80,000 volumes on Italian and foreign productions, drama, criticism and the history of the theater.

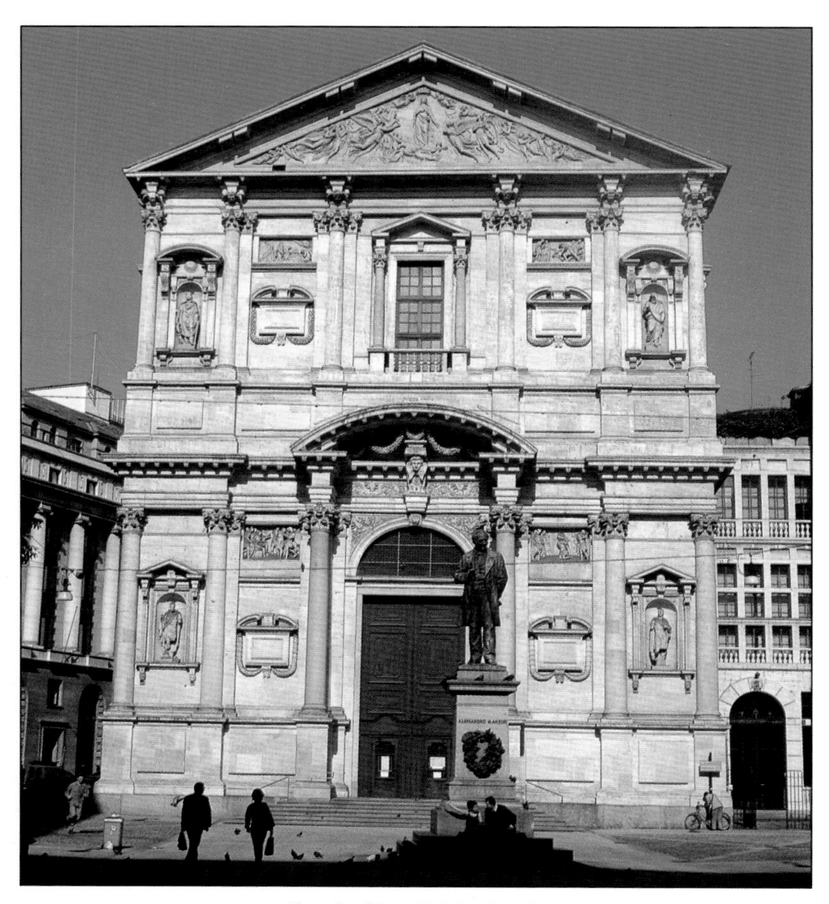

Church of San Fedele, façade

Church of San Fedele

The church is situated in the plaza of the same name, where the *Monument to Alessandro Manzoni* by Francesco Barzaghi stands (1883). The building of the church was begun in 1569 by Pellegrini for San Carlo Borromeo. It was then continued by Martino Bassi and Richini and eventually finished in the 19th century. The façade is typically 16th century in its decoration and architecture. It was badly damaged by the bombings in the last war and was later restored. The relief of the *Assumption* in the tympanum is by Monti.

The **interior** has a single nave, divided into two spans supported by columns placed against the walls; there are several good paintings including, on the first altar to the right, *Saint Ignatius Gloriosus* by Cerano; the second altar has a curious set of columns supported by *Angels* and *Four Saints* by Bernardino Campi;

Casa degli Omenoni, detail of the façade

House of Alessandro Manzoni

the first altar to the left, *Deposition* by Simone Peterzano. The beautiful 16th century inlaid confessionals, are the work of the Taurinis, while the wooden inlaid choir-stall near the apse, which comes from the demolished church of S. Maria della Scala, is attributed to Anselmo Del Conte (16th century). The *sacristy* with its stupendous inlaid wardrobes (entrance after the second altar to the right) is said to be the most beautiful in Milan .

Palazzo Belgioioso

Behind the church of San Fedele runs the narrow Via Omenoni, which gets its name from the 16th century house at no. 3, called **Casa degli Omenoni** (house of the big men) because of the eight gigantic *caryatids* that adorn the lower part of the façade. This beautiful house was built in the second half of the 16th century by the sculptor Leone Leoni for his own use. The via Omenoni leads to the picturesque and secluded Piazza Belgioioso with, to the right, the imposing Neoclassic *Palazzo Belgioioso* constructed by Giuseppe Piermarini (1772-81) and commissioned by Prince Alberico XII Belgioioso. The building opposite is *Palazzo Besana*, built in 1815, while the brick house at the end, at the corner of Via Morone, is the **House of Alessandro Manzoni**, where the writer lived from 1814 until his death on the 22nd of May, 1873.

Today it is the *National Center for Studies on Manzoni* and the *Manzoni Museum*, which includes the poet's study with its furniture and books, the bedroom where he died, and a collection of sketches, memorabilia and books. Via Morone leads into via Alessandro Manzoni, where immediately to the right, in an imposing building at no. 12, we find the entrance to the Poldi-Pezzoli Museum.

Poldi-Pezzoli Museum

The Museum contains the remarkable art collection that the nobleman Gian Giacomo Poldi-Pezzoli, one of the most knowledgeable and enthusiastic art collectors of the 19th century, assembled in his residence. The number and quality of the works of art in the collection bear witness to the discernment and commitment of this private collector. At his death (1879) he willed the precious collection to the city.

The Interior - The ground floor beyond the entrance, where *the Portrait of Gian Giacomo Poldi-Pezzoli* by Francesco Hayez is displayed, houses the **Armory** which has a collection of firearms, halberds, swords, daggers etc.; the **Fresco Hall**, with the magnificent *Delft tapestry*, with scenes of chivalry (1602), the hood from a Bishop's Cope based on designs by Botticelli, frontals of altars of the 15th century and marvelous Venetian mirrors; the **Archeological and Carpet Room**, with fragments of Coptic textiles, the Täbriz Carpet (around 1560) vases, bronzes, silver-ware, gold, and bronze and iron-age weapons. Returning to the entrance, one climbs the picturesque **staircase** with the Baroque marble fountain by Petiti at the bottom and, on the wall, the great *Landscapes* by Alessandro Magnasco, and 17th century statues. On the first floor in the vestibule, *Bust of Count Meipperg* by Canova and *Bust of Rosa Poldi-Pezzoli* by Lorenzo Bartolini; among the paintings, *Allegory* by Giulio Campi.

The building where the Poldi-Pezzoli Museum is located, in Via A. Manzoni

Poldi-Pezzoli Museum, Portrait of a Young Woman, formerly attributed to A. Pollaiolo (Golden Room)

From here one passes into the three **Rooms of the Lombards** which display the works of Lombard Masters of the Renaissance, among which the most important are: *Madonna with Child* a masterpiece by Vincenzo Foppa to whom the *Portrait of Francesco Brivio* is also attributed; *Madonna Suckling the Child* and *Rest during the Flight to Egypt* by Andrea Solario of whom there are also two other works; *Madonna and Child Picking a Flower*, masterpiece by Giovanni Antonio Boltraffio; *the Mystic Wedding of Saint Catherine* by Bernardino Luini and other works by this painter; *Madonna and Saints* by Gaudenzio Ferrari, and together with other paintings, there is a precious painted wooden sculpture of the 16th century, the *Marriage of the Virgin*. Returning to the vestibule, one enters the **Room of the Foreigners** with *Landscape* and *Genre Scenes* by Jan Brueghel the Elder and four small tablet paintings by Lucas Cranach the Elder with the *Portrait of Martin Luther* and of *Kate von Bora, St. John the Baptist* and the *Immaculate Conception*. There follows the **Stucco-work Room** which is decorated in 18th century style with a small Saxony porcelain statue of *Augustus the Strong*. In the glass case there is a precious collection of porcelain from Saxony, Vienna, Capodimonte and Sèvres. In the **Golden Room**, the most famous and valuable works belonging to the Museum are displayed. On the floor lies the famous Persian carpet with hunting scenes dated 1523. Among the numerous paintings the following are particularly noteworthy: *Madonna and Child* by Andrea Mantegna; *Lament over the Dead Christ* by Giovanni Bellini; *Madonna and Child* and *Lament over the Dead Christ*, two paintings by Sandro Botticelli; *St. Nicholas of Tolentino* by Piero della Francesca; *Portrait of a Young Woman*, a masterpiece formerly attributed to Antonio Pollaiolo and now thought to be by his brother Piero; *Grey Lagoon* by Francesco Guardi. In addition we find works by Bartolomeo Montagna, Antonio Vivarini and a magnificent bronze bust by Gian Lorenzo Bernini representing the *Bishop Ulpiano Volpi*. At the far end in the **Romanelli Room**, which takes its name from the Antwerp tapestry, based on a design by G. Francesco Romanelli, we find, besides paintings by Maratta, Bernardo Cavallino and others, a wooden Tuscan *Crucifix* of the 14th century. Returning to the Golden Room, we find the entrance to the **Black Room** with a 17th century table in marble marquetry work from the Florentine Opificio delle Pietre Dure (where table tops and oth-

er objects were made of semi-precious stones). In the corner is the famous sculpture by Lorenzo Bartolini, *Faith in God.* Among the numerous paintings are the *Triptych* by Mariotto Albertinelli; *Faith* by Luca Signorelli*; St. Catherine of Alexandria* by Bergognone; *Portrait of Cardinal Carlo de' Medici,* by Sustermans. In the following **Murano Glass Room**, there is an exceptional collection of 15th to 19th century glass, displayed in two large cases. Among the paintings we note the *Annunciation* by Francesco Pesellino; *Madonna and Child with Saints* by Sodoma; various miniatures by artists from Florence, Umbria, and the Marches (15th century) and two Tyrolean painted wooden bas-reliefs (16th century). Through the two doors one passes to the **Dante Room** decorated in Neo-Gothic floral style of the late 19th century. In the glass cases: Wedgewood ceramics, Oriental porcelain, and silver. In the central glass case *Dante* by Giuseppe Bertini. Returning to the Black Room one passes into the **Tapestry Room** which takes its name from the tapestry with a scene of *Knights in Battle.* In this room there are various interesting paintings including: *San Carlo Borromeo receives the Oblates* by Alessandro Magnasco; *Portrait* by Giuseppe Ribera; the *Death of St. Jerome, Joshua stops the Sun* and *Strength and Wisdom,* three works by G. Battista Tiepolo and other works by Bernardo Strozzi, Francesco Morazzone, Francesco Guardi, Palma il Vecchio, Luca Giordano. There follows the **Goldwork Cabinet** with a precious collection of jewels, diadems, diamonds and golden objects and figurines, gold and silver caskets, etc. In the **Room of Ghislandi**, known also as Friar Galgario, we find one of his masterpieces*: Gentleman with a Three-cornered Hat.* The other works are by Francesco Zuccarelli, Domenico Feti, Rosalba Carriera, Francesco Guardi, Bernardo Bellotto and others. In the **Room of Perugino** by whom *Madonna with Angels* was painted, there are other works by artists of the Veneto, Emilia, Tuscany and Umbria. *Madonna and Child, Angels and Saints* by Pietro Lorenzetti; *St. Maurelius* by Cosmè Tura*; Samson and Delilah* by Francesco Morone; *Crucifixion* by Giovanni Bellini*; Lament over the Dead Christ* by Filippo Lippi; *St. Jerome* by Antoniazzo Romano as well as works by Bartolomeo di Giovanni, Carlo Crivelli, Francesco Bonsignori. In the **Venetian Room** we find one of the best works of Cima da Conegliano

Poldi-Pezzoli Museum, Madonna and Child by Cristoforo Moretti

with the *Triumph of Bacchus and Arianna*, and also *Head of a Saint.* We also find other works by artists of the Venetian Renaissance including *The Holy Family with St. John and St. Catherine,* two works by L. Lotto; the *Annunciation* by M. Palmezzano; *the Visit of the Doctor* by Bonifazio de' Pitati and others by artists of the school of Carpaccio and Mantegna. On the terrace there is a marble statuary group by Lorenzo Bartolini, *Pyrrhus Throwing Astyanax from the Tower as Andromache Looks On.*

Via Manzoni is one of the liveliest of the main thoroughfares of Milan, with 19th century houses on either side which have been made into attractive hotels, banks, insurance companies and beautiful shops. At no. 11 we find the 16th century **Palazzo Bigli** with ornate portals, and pendentives with two medallions in relief of the *Annunciation.* After the entrance into via Montenapoleone (on the right) we find the 18th century **Church of S. Francesco da Paola**: the street continues until at the end, we reach the **Arches of Porta Nuova** (New Gate), with two barrel-vaults of black and white marble which were once part of the city walls built to defend the town from Barbarossa in 1156. On the external façade there is a marble tabernacle with the *Madonna and Child between Saints Ambrose, Gervase and Protase,* in the manner of Giovanni di Balduccio, placed there by Azzone Visconti in the 14th century, while on the inside there are busts in niches, stone grave markers and funeral plaques. Turning back we proceed along **Via Montenapoleone** which is the most aristocratic street of Milan with 19th century houses, some of which are Neoclassical. It is lined on either side with luxury shops, especially antique shops. Many of the streets which lead to the 19th century neighborhoods of Milan start here; the fourth to the left is via Sant'Andrea where, at no. 6, we find the 18th century *Palazzo Morando Attendolo Bolognini,* which contains the

Arches of Porta Nuova

Via Montenapoleone

Civic Museum of Contemporary History inaugurated in 1963, the **Milan Museum** founded in 1935 and the **Mursia Museum of Marine Art**. Via Montenapoleone leads into Corso Matteotti to the right, and the lively piazza San Babila to the left which is the meeting point of several important streets. It is surrounded by tall modern buildings with porticos and at the end the *Colonna del Leone* (Column of the Lion - 1626) and on the right of the square, the **Basilica of San Babila** built in the 11thcentury, but much altered since Alessandro Manzoni was baptized in this church on August 8th, 1785, as the commemorative plaque informs us. We continue along Corso Vittorio Emanuele which was almost totally reconstructed after the damage suffered during the war. This is a very lively street with porticos on either side, luxury shops of various kinds and cafes. This street leads to the northern side of Piazza del Duomo. At the end of the porticoed arcade, we take Via Mercanti, flanked on the right by **Palazzo dei Giureconsulti** built in 1562 by the architect Vincenzo Seregni for Pope Pius IV (Angelo Maria Medici, who was a Milanese). The façade was designed by Galeazzo Alessi. The building which has a multi-level base, a twin-columned portico,

Basilica of San Babila

Palazzo della Ragione or Broletto Nuovo

Palazzo dei Giureconsulti

elegant windows and a tower built in 1272. The statue on the ground floor of *St. Ambrose* by Luigi Scorzini replaces the original statue of Philip II which was transformed into Brutus during the French Revolution. On the other side lies the **Palazzo della Ragione** (Palace of Reason) or **Broletto Nuovo**, the most

Piazza Mercanti

Loggia degli Osii

remarkable building of the Free Commune and Romanesque period. Built in 1233, it has a raised ground floor, with open archways upon pillars and three-mullioned windows on the first floor; in 1771 a second floor was added. On the side which looks onto the piazza, there is a Romanesque high-relief which shows the first podestà of Milan *Oldrado da Tresseno* on horseback, by Benedetto Antelami, placed here by the Commune in 1233. The picturesque **Piazza Mercanti** which originally formed a closed quadrangle was once the true heart of Medieval Milan and even today is surrounded by many important monuments. In front of the Palazzo della Ragione there is the **Palazzo delle Scuole Palatine** (Palace of the Palatine Schools) built in 1645 by Carlo Buzzi who used the same architectural motifs as the Palazzo dei Giureconsulti. The statue above the arch, shows the *poet Ausonius* (died 394) who wrote verses in praise of Milan. To the left of the palazzo, the **Loggia degli Osii** which Matteo Visconti had built in 1316 by Scoto da S. Gemignano. It is made of black and white marble, with two open porticoes one on top of the other. The upper part is decorated with graceful three-mullioned niches which contain nine 14th century statues of the *Madonna and Saints.* Along the parapet of the upper loggia are to be seen the arms and devices of the Viscontis and the various quarters of Medieval Milan.

Castello Sforzesco

At the northern corner of Piazza del Duomo, where the Northern Arcade ends, one takes Via dei Mercanti which is flanked to the right by Palazzo dei Giureconsulti and to the left by Palazzo della Ragione. The road ends in Piazza Cordusio, at the center of which rises the bronze *Monument to Giuseppe Parini* by Luigi Secchi (1899). After having crossed the square, we go straight down Via Dante, one of the most lively thoroughfares of the city with its large buildings, to which the tower of the Castle acts as a back-drop. The street ends in Largo Cairoli with the *Monument to Giuseppe Garibaldi* by Ettore Ximenes (1895) in the middle. To the right and left of Largo Cairoli, large avenues lined with trees begin, forming a semi-circle around the Sforza Castle known as Foro Buonaparte. From behind the monument via Beltrami leads to the grand Castle square (Piazza Castello) with its vast flower beds and trees.

Castello Sforzesco

This grandiose structure, which is one of the most extraordinary civic monuments of the Renaissance period, was started in the 14th century, when Galeazzo II Visconti ordered construction of the building to begin as a stronghold and the name of *Castle of the Jovian Gate* was given to it since it was in the vicinity of Porta Giovia (the Jovian Gate of the Roman wall). It also incorporated a part of the wall into its structure. It was then extended by his successors, Gian Galeazzo, Giovanni Maria and finally by Filippo Maria, who had it altered and improved with the help of the architect Filippo Brunelleschi, as he wished it to be used as the permanent residence for the Visconti dynasty. After the death of Duke Filippo Maria in 1447, the fortress was sacked by proponents of the Ambrosian Republic who had taken over the government of the city. In 1450, the soldier of fortune or *condottiero* Fran-

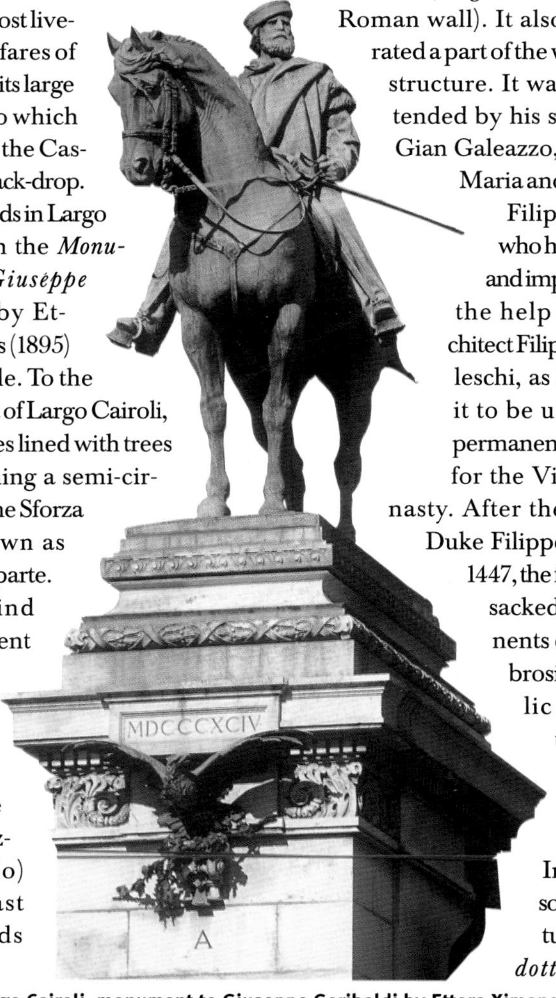

MDCCCXCIV

A

Largo Cairoli, monument to Giuseppe Garibaldi by Ettore Ximenes

Castello Sforzesco, aerial view

cesco Sforza, after the fall of the Republic, took possession of the stronghold. He began the reconstruction with the intention of creating a fortification for his own defense but it was gradually transformed into an architectural structure which had the appearance of a noble residence. To start with, the work was entrusted to Giovanni da Milano with the assistance of Filippo Scorzioli and, in 1451, the direction of the works continued under Jacopo da Cortona. In 1452 the Prince engaged the Florentine architect Filarete to construct and decorate the middle tower of the castle which, however, was begun two years later, when work on the building under the direction of Bartolomeo Gadio of Cremona resumed. After the death of Francesco Sforza (1466), his son Galeazzo Maria succeeded him and work was continued under the direction of another Florentine architect, Benedetto Ferrini, to whom we owe the loggia, the great staircase, the portico of the Elephant, the chapel and the back portion of the Rocchetta. The decoration of the Castle was entrusted to painters of the Dukedom of Milan. Under the regency of Bona di Savoia, the tower to which she gave her name was built (1476). With the rise to power of Ludovico il Moro (1494), the fourth son of Francesco Sforza, the castle became one of the most splendid residences in Italy: it was decorated by Bramante, and the great Leonardo da Vinci and numerous other artists were summoned to work there. After Ludovico il Moro's fall (1499), the magnificent palace was occupied by the French forces commanded by Marshal Gian Giacomo Trivulzio and the deterioration of the splendid castle commenced. In 1521, a gun powder explosion caused the destruction of the central tower

Castello Sforzesco, detail of the outside

built by Filarete. During the Spanish domination (16th-17th century) the castle underwent further transformation and addition of buildings, becoming a military fortress. Charles V had a new rampart built which connected it to the new walls of the city. At the end of the 16th century the stronghold was surrounded by six bulwarks. At the beginning of the 17th century the moat and the covered road along the external border were built.

Entrance to the Castello Sforzesco

In 1707 the Spaniards finally capitulated to General Koenigseck. In 1733, the fortress was conquered by Carlo Emanuel III of Savoy at the head of the Franco-Sardinian troops. In 1746 the fortress was occupied once more by the Spaniards for a short time. In 1796 it was conquered by the French and in 1799 by the Russians under the command of Field Marshal Suvaroff. After the Austrians had abandoned the fortress, Napoleon demolished the Spanish additions and only the original Castello Sforzesco was left standing. In 1814 the Austrians returned and during the epic battle known as the "*Five Days*", in March of 1845, Radetzky withdrew into the Castle with his general staff and his troops and from here bombarded the city and ordered the demolition of the corner towers. After the liberation of Lombardy the old castle became a barracks and in 1880 was supposed to be torn down. During the following years, however, a large number of Milanese, and the intervention of

Castello Sforzesco, Statue of St. Ambrose on the Filarete tower

Castello Sforzesco, Filarete tower

the *Lombard Historical Society*, foiled all attempts in this direction, to the extent that, in 1893, the architect Luca Beltrami, who had already submitted a project, began a radical reconstruction. In the three main structures which constitute the historic building - the *Parade Ground*, the *Rocchetta* and the *Ducal Court* he located the *Civic Institutes for Art and History.* Although it was damaged once more during the last war, the Sforza Castle

Castello Sforzesco, detail of the courtyard of the Parade Ground

was restored and became a museum.

Outside of the Castle - At the center of the façade with its front towards the city, rises the so-called *Filarete Tower* (called also *Torre dell'Orologio* or *Clock Tower*) which is 227 feet high. It was reconstructed at the beginning of the 20th century by the architect Luca Beltrami, and was restored to the appearance it had had before being destroyed in 1521. It is a square tower

Castello Sforzesco, Courtyard of the Parade Ground

with two upper stories, each of which is smaller than that below, culminating in a small cupola. Above the great door is a bas-relief by Luigi Secchi representing *King Umberto II on horseback* (1916). Higher-up, under the first battlements is *St. Ambrose* amidst the coats of arms of the six Sforza dukes. Six magnificently ornamented and richly decorated marble and brick mullioned windows are set into the massive front walls of the castle, which stretch out left and right from the Central Clock tower, leading to the two massive cylindrical corner towers in rough-hewn blocks of stone. They are 100 feet high, crowned with battlements and decorated with the great marble coat of arms with the *Visconti-Sforza emblem* of the *grass-snake*. The sides and the rear have the same characteristics as the façade. At the level of the Rocchetta and the Ducal Court are two series of large Gothic windows decorated with brickwork frames. The corner towers at the back are the *Torre Falconiera* to the right and the *Torre Castellana* (or *Tower of the Treasure*) to the left; they are square structures with large windows. At the center of the side facing the Park there is a great doorway called the *Porta del Barco*. On the left side, next to *Porta Santo Spirito*, are the picturesque restored ruins of a ravelin. On the right is the *Porta dei*

Castello Sforzesco, Courtyard of the Ducal Court

Carmini with a drawbridge and the *bridge of Ludovico il Moro* which crosses over the moat and leads to a handsome little loggia which has been attributed to Bramante.

Interior - The doorway, under the tower of Filarete, leads into the grandiose and picturesque **Parade Ground** (Piazza d'Armi), now a garden, which was once used for marching by the Sforza troops. The front of the tower on the inside is distinguished by a balcony with a three-mullioned window, while along the left side of the wall runs a structure which acts as a support. The end of the courtyard is closed by three buildings with a dry moat in front of them; to the left stands the **Rocchetta**, a fortified building in which the Sforzas took refuge in times of danger; in the center stands the **Tower of Bona di Savoia**, which is 117 feet high and was commissioned by the widow of Galeazzo Maria Sforza in 1477; to the right, the palace of the **Ducal Court**, the residence of the Sforzas in times of peace. The solitary statue in front of the moat is *St. John Nepomucenus*, erected in 1729. At the sides of the great square there are two doors with a drawbridge that crosses the external moat; the door on the right is the *Porta dei Carmini*, decorated with architectural fragments of different epochs; the one on the left is the *Porta di Santo Spirito* (Door of the Holy Spirit).

The Ducal Court - Access to the court is through the door surmounted by a great Sforza coat-of-arms, which stands upon the site of the old Jovian Gate and leads into the Vestibule where sculptures and fragments of various Milanese buildings are kept. On the wall one can still see the fresco of the *Crucifix between Saints* by an anonymous Lombard painter (1470-80) showing the artist's patron, Ambrosiano da Longhignana, who was at that time the keeper of the castle for Galeazzo Maria Sforza and Bona di Savoia. From the vestibule one enters the stupendous **Courtyard** of the Ducal Court, flanked on three sides by a one story construction with two levels of ogival windows. The ground floor of the end wall is graced by the Renaissance "*Elephant Portico*", which owes its name to the elephant painted on the wall, by Benedetto Ferrini (1473) who also designed the graceful two-storied loggia at the beginning of the left wing, called the *Loggia of Galeazzo Maria*, that stands above the vestibule of the great staircase.

The Art Museums - One enters the

museums from the right wing of the courtyard. The collections are arranged in the old rooms which have been renovated according to modern museum standards, and include sculptures, paintings, furniture and tapestries, musical instruments, works of art in gold, ivory, glass and ceramics. On the ground floor we find the **Sculpture Museum**, which contains prevalently Lombard works, but also has fine examples of late Roman and Byzantine art. On the upper floor there is a collection of furniture with examples which range from late Gothic chests of the 15th century to lacquered Venetian trumeaux of the 18th century. The **Picture Gallery** also displays prevalently Lombard works, and boasts a variety of paintings by great artists of various epochs. In the Rooms of the Rocchetta, ceramics, gold, bronzes, ivory, wrought iron and glass are displayed. In addition, in the adjacent rooms we find the **Museum of Antique Musical Instruments**, which, for the extraordinary variety of its collection, is considered unique in all of Europe. The list that follows mentions only the most significant of the many objects that are contained in the 32 rooms.

Room I - (Early Christian and pre-Romanesque art) - Past the entrance and before entering the Museum, we find the *Blacksmith's Postern* which was part of the 14th century Visconti wall. Here are displayed fragments of mosaic floors, frescoes from tombs, various architectural fragments, capitals, sarcophagi, and sculptures which date from the 4th to the 9th century. Of particular interest: fragment of an early *Christian sarcophagus* with male and female figures, of the 4th century; a 6th century fresco from a tomb with a jewel encrusted *Cross and Deer*, from the church of S. Giovanni in Conca; head in marble, perhaps of the *Empress Theodora*, of the 6th century; fragment of a head (11th century) from the Baptistery of St. John in Florence.

Room II - (Romanesque and Campionese art) - This room contains the *Sepulchral Monument* and *Equestrian Statue of Bernabò Visconti*, from the church of S. Giovanni in Conca. The statue is by Bonino da Campione (1370-80). On the walls are reliefs and fragments of the 13th century; wooden *Crucifix* of the 13th century.; relief of *Christ Giving His Benediction*, *Sarcophagus of Giovanni da Fagnano*; the front of the *sarcophagus of Vieri da Bassignana* of the 14th century; the *sepulchral monument of Regina della Scala*, the wife of Bernabò Visconti, of the 14th century. In the lunettes and on the wall at the end we find various coats-of-arms of Spanish governors.

Room III - The fresco on the vault representing the *Resurrection* is by an anonymous 15th century Lombard artist. The borders of the vaults are decorated with coats-of-arms of the dukedom. Along the wall are: a statue of *St. James the Greater* (14th century), the front of the *sarcophagus of friar Mirano di Bachaloe*, Campionese art; statue of *Madonna and Child and St. Ambrose* which decorated the tabernacles of the Porta Comacina, a *Madonna between Saints Babila, Ambrose, Benedict and Dionysius* which

Castello Sforzesco, Funeral monument to Bernabò Visconti, by Bonino da Campione (Art Museums - Room II)

comes from the Malatesta Temple in Rimini, is the most interesting.
Room XII - The ducal chapel was decorated in 1466-76 by Stefano de' Fedeli and assistants, by order of Galeazzo Maria Sforza. On the vault is a *Resurrection*; in the lunettes the *Annunciation* and coats-of-arms; along the walls, *Saints*. In the center of the room, a statue known as the *Coazzone* or *Praying Madonna*, a work attributed to Pietro Solari. In addition, *Madonna and Child* on a small pedestal supported by cherubs, and an *Angel*, Gothic art of the 15th century, also *Angel Musicians*, in the style of Amadeo.
Room XIII - Known also as the *Sala delle Colombine* (Room of the Doves) on account of its frescoes adorned with gold roundels and doves against a red background, which Bona di Savoia had painted. Among the various Lombard sculptures are *Angels and Anchorites* by Cristoforo Mantegazza and *Angels* by Amadeo. The two 15th century portals facing each other between this room and the next are also interesting.
Room XIV - Known as the *Green Room* because it was originally painted green. Here the visitor can admire a fine series of Renaissance portals including the magnificent marble *Portal of the Medici Bank* by the Florentine, Michelozzo (1455) is of major interest. In addition, the Roman *Orsini Portal* of the 16th century; the *Bentivoglio Portal* of the 16th century, capitals from the *Portico of Figini* (15th century) which come from Piazza del Duomo are worthy of note. In the glass case are Lombard and Renaissance weapons, and 16th century Italian and German armor.

Castello Sforzesco, room housing the Civic Collection of Arms

Room XV - Known as the *Room of the Scarlioni* on account of the arrow-like stripes painted in red on the wall, of which only traces remain. Here the secret councils were held and it was also used as an audience hall. The room is divided into two parts; in the first one the *Statue of Gaston de Foix Lying in Death*, by Bambaia who worked on it along with his brother until 1525, and the great *Funeral monument of the Bishop Bagaroto* by Andrea Fusina (1519).
In the second part a staircase leads to a niche enshrining the famous *Pietà Rondanini* by Michelangelo, his last work, left unfinished.
One leaves this room through a small door at the end and crosses the *Courtyard of the Fountain* by means of a wooden walkway. In the courtyard, a copy of the ancient marble fountain of the Sforzas (the original is in the cathedral of Bellinzona). To the right, the staircase, also known as *the Scala Cavallina* (Stair of the Little Horse) leads to the floor above.
Room XVI - Known also as the *Upper Green Room* where the great receptions were held in the time of the dukedom. This room is divided into four completely independent sections which are not in communication with each other and which can be reached only by going out and entering from the next room. Among the many things in the first section are: the 15th century inlaid marriage chest, called the *Cassone delle Torri*; a very rare wooden choir screen called the *Coretto of Torrechiara* (15th century). Among the frescoes on the walls the *Crucifixion* is worthy of mention.
Room XVII - Besides furniture, this room contains an important series of frescoes of the Lombard school. *Allegorical figures* of the 15th and 16th centuries

Castello Sforzesco, the Pietà Rondanini (Art Museums - Room XV)

Castello Sforzesco, Stories of Griselda, attr. to Nicolò da Varallo (Art Museums - Room XVII)

and *Episodes from the Life of Jesus* (15th century). In the center is a remarkable reconstruction of the series of frescoes representing the *Stories of Griselda* from the castle of Roccabianca, a work attributed to Nicolò da Varallo. From here one enters the two sections of Room XVI, where marriage chests, beds, wardrobes and bureaus are exhibited with cabinets, caskets. Upon a great Tuscan table of the 16th century stands a *basin* of chiseled and cast bronze, a beautiful work by Leone Leoni. On the walls there are 17th century tapestries from Antwerp and Brussels.

Room XVIII (17th century furniture) - The most precious of the pieces of furniture is the celebrated *Passalacqua Casket* of 1613, a beautiful coffer embellished with ivory, bronze, and paintings by Morazzone. From here one enters the last section of Room XVI, containing Venetian furniture of the 18th century and two sedan chairs one of which is a lavishly decorated Neapolitan model. On the walls are paintings including the *Procession of the Imperial Ambassador Clerici* by the Florentine Antonio Cioci (1759) and *Portrait of a Great Lady* attributed to Alessandro Longhi. The chandelier is made of Venetian glass from Murano.

Room XIX - This room contains 18th century furniture from various places. Of great interest is the Piedmontese chest of drawers a *rocailles* with a Viennese clock on it; the four Lombard arm chairs are covered with tapestry upholstery and the chest of drawers is decorated in bronze with a marble group upon it representing *Aeneas, An-*

Castello Sforzesco, armchair (furniture collection on the upper floor)

chises and *Ascanius*. Valuable paintings are on the walls.

Room XX - This room, known also as the *Golden Room*, and the following six rooms contain the Picture Gallery. Among the many works on display here of the various schools of the 14th-15th centuries, the following are particularly interesting: *Madonna and Child between Saints and Angels* by Filippo Lippi; *Madonna and Child* by Giovanni Bellini and *Poet Laureate* also attributed to Bellini. The great tempera in the middle of the room, the *Madonna in Glory among Saints*, is by Andrea Mantegna (1497).

Room XXI - The room contains works by Lombard painters of the 15th - 16th centuries. By Bergognone there is a *Deposition, St. Benedict giving Alms, St. Jerome and St. Roch.* By Foppa: two *Holy Bishops*, the famous *St. Sebastian*, the *Madonna of the Book*, the *Madonna Trivulzio, St. Francis and St. John the Baptist*. Also: a *Madonna* by Bernardino Luini; *Portrait of a Woman*, by Giovanni Antonio Boltraffio; *St. Michael* by Sodoma and other works by R. Moretto, Bramantino, De Predis and others.
Room XXII - This little hall contains a number of small format Mannerist paintings.
Room XXIII - Lombard paintings from the Chapel of the Tribunale di Provvisione (the town's main administrative board). Works by Salmeggia, Nuvolone, Figino, and others and a very interesting *Pentecost* by Morazzone.
Room XXIV - Italian Mannerists of Northern Italy. A particularly fine *Martyrdom of St. Sebastian* by A. Campi (1575) and various works by Procaccini. The door adorned with crests and medallions comes from the house that was given to Lucia Marliani by Galeazzo Maria Sforza in 1474.
Room XXV - The Lombard Region Room. - Works normally stored in the Museum deposits take turns being exhibited in this room. The shows are set up according to various themes and give the visitor the possibility of seeing works which are often of exceptional quality and interest.
Room XXVI - 17th and 18th century paintings. The Lombard works are separated from the other schools. Of particular interest: *St. Michael Archangel* by Cerano, *St. Charles Fasting* by Danilo Crespi, two *Storms* by Alessandro Magnasco, *Portrait of a Young Man* by Fra' Galgario, *St. Francis in Ecstasy* by Francesco del Cairo, *Storm at Sea* by F. Guardi.
The small door at the end of the great hall leads to a little bridge which crosses over the upper part of the Tower of Bona di Savoia, and leads eventually to the rooms on the upper floor of the Rocchetta, where the ceramics, and objects of gold and ivory are displayed. Past rooms XXVII and XXVIII (the latter contains wrought iron objects) is the enormous **Ceramics Section** which occupies three rooms. In the first (XXIX) one finds decorative and figurative pottery and several examples of incised slipware. In the second room (XXX) which is divided into sections, the statues attributed to G. di Balduccio da Pisa and the portraits of personalities from the Visconti and Sforza families are interesting. The Chinese pottery, the 15th - 17th century majolica from Faenza, Urbino, Savona, Albisola, Angarano, Castelli d'Abruzzo and the pottery of Milan and Lodi in the glass cases, are all worthy of note. In the third room (XXXI) there are examples of Italian and foreign pottery of the 18th and 19th centuries. Also, porcelain from Vienna, Doccia, Capodimonte, Meissen, Venice and Sèvres.
Room XXXII is devoted to gold, ivory and bronze objects. Among these, the *Gothic monstrance* of 1456, the 15th century *Stories of the Passion*, and the two beautiful caravels are the most interesting. Among the ivory works are the famous tablets with the *Two Marys at the Sepulcher*, Roman art of the 5th century, and the diptych of the *Console Magno*, Byzantine art of the 6th cen-

Castello Sforzesco, display cases in one of the rooms of the Museum of Antique Musical Instruments

tury; precious Murano glass and various bronze objects of interest.
The rooms of the lower floor around the Rocchetta are devoted to Hellenistic and Coptic textiles of the 2nd to the 8th century and to liturgical hangings, costumes etc., and to the **Museum of Antique Musical Instruments** founded in 1958 and opened to the public in 1963. This collection of 641 pieces is the only one of its kind in Europe. It contains string, plucked, keyboard and wind instruments arranged in such a way as to give an idea of the history of musical instruments over five centuries, from the 15th century to modern times. All the instruments are of great interest either because they are works of master craftsmen such as Gasparo da Salò, Guarnieri, or Stradivarius, or on account of their great artistic value. On the same floor there is the Sala della Bella (which is normally closed since it is reserved for receptions and ceremonies) where we find the 12 famous tapestries with the *Allegories of the Months*, made for Marshal Trivulzio in 1503 to designs by Bramantino, by the ducal tapestry weavers of Vigevano.

The Courtyard of the Rocchetta - The courtyard is reached by going down the great austere staircase. The Rocchetta is a fortress within a fortress surrounded on three sides by porti-

Castello Sforzesco, Courtyard of the Rocchetta

coes; the right one was constructed by the Florentine Benedetto Ferrini (1466-76) by order of Gian Galeazzo Maria, the one opposite is by Filarete and the left one was begun by Bernardino da Corte in 1495 and finished by Bramante by order of Ludovico il Moro. From the Courtyard, through an archway, one enters the **Treasure Room**, so called because the ducal treasure was kept there, with frescoes of the Lombard school and a damaged fresco by Bramante on one of the walls, showing *Argus* with his hundred eyes guarding the door leading to a small room in which the most precious jewels of the Duke were kept. Two sections of the **Municipal Archeology and**

Castello Sforzesco, seen from the Sempione Park

Male profile, Egyptian bas-relief carving (Egyptian Museum -Courtyard of the Rocchetta)

Monument to Napoleon III in the Sempione Park

Numismatic Collections are housed in the museum section of the Castello Sforzesco and these include objects relating to prehistory, Egyptian history and the history of coins from the 6th century B.C. to modern times.
Leaving the Castle by the gate called the *Porta del Barco* across the moat, the **Sempione Park** lies directly ahead. It is a vast English style garden which takes up an area of 47 hectares and includes picturesque groups of trees, green lawns and flower beds. In the background we see the *Arch of Peace* (Arco della Pace). To the right we take via Gadio to get to the **Civic Aquarium** and behind it, at the edge of the park, is the oval of the Neoclassical **Arena** or *Civic Stadium* designed by Luigi Canonica and inaugurated in 1807 in the presence of Napoleon. In the Arena, which nowadays is used for competitive sports, horse races and chariot races were once held. Within the boundaries of the park there is also the **Palazzo dell'Arte** (the Palace of the Arts) which has recently been restored for use as an exhibition hall. The *Gallery of the Triennale* which houses the triennial exhibition was redesigned by architect G. Aulenti in the 1950s. On the knoll known as the *Monte Tondo* we can see the *Monument to Napoleon III* by Francesco Barzaghi (1881). Spacious Piazza Sempione lies on the far side of the park.

Funerary mask made of plaster with eyes of glass paste, Roman era (Egyptian Museum - Courtyard of the Rocchetta)

Arch of Peace

Arch of Peace

The Arch is one of the most characteristic monuments in Milan. It was begun in 1807 by the Neoclassical artist, Luigi Cagnola for the purpose of creating a monument to celebrate the exploits of Napoleon I, an intention which was foiled by subsequent political events. In fact, in 1826, the monument was dedicated to Francis I of Austria and called the *Arch of Peace* to commemorate the Peace of Europe of 1815. Later, in 1859, it was used to commemorate the entry of Victor Emmanuel II and Napoleon III into Milan. The monument, which is 81 feet high, is composed of 3 arches with 4 great columns on each side and is surmounted by the great bronze *Chariot of Peace Drawn by Six Horses* by Abbondio Sangiorgio while the four *Victories on horseback* at the corners are by G. Patti. Above the pediment, the four principal rivers of Lombardy and the Veneto are represented: the *Po*, the *Ticino*, the *Adige* and the *Tagliamento*. The reliefs on the two façades show *Episodes of the Restoration after the Fall of Napoleon.*

Third Itinerary

1 The Brera Palace (with the Brera Art Gallery)
2 Church of San Marco
3 Royal Villa (with the Gallery of Modern Art)
4 Public Gardens

To get to the Brera Art Gallery it is best to begin from Piazza della Scala, taking via Giuseppe Verdi where one can admire the elegant baroque façade of the **Church of San Giuseppe** on the right, one of the finest architectural achievements of Francesco M. Richini (1630). The road continues until it gets to via Brera, a typical Milanese street, flanked by Neoclassical and 18th century buildings including, on the left, at no. 15, the *Palazzo Cusani* by Giovanni Ruggeri (1719). On the right, at no. 28, we find the *Brera Palace.*

The Brera Palace, Courtyard with the bronze statue of Napoleon I by A. Canova

The Brera Palace
Palazzo di Brera

This monumental building was built by the Jesuits on the site of a pre-existing monastery of the Humiliated Brethren. The job of designing the palace was given to Francesco Maria Richini, who worked on the project from 1651 until his death in 1658. His son Gian Domenico continued work on the project and others followed until it was finally completed in 1773. The great portal was added in 1780 by Piermarini. The entrance hall leads into a superb rectangular courtyard with two rows of arches supported by twin columns, an architectural masterpiece by Richini based upon designs by Martino Bassi. At the center of the courtyard is a bronze statue of *Napoleon I*, by Antonio Canova (1809). The emperor bears the symbol of victory in his right hand and the scepter of command in his left hand. Statues and busts representing illustrious personalities of the arts and sciences who took part in the life of Milan, are to be found between the surrounding columns. After the suppression of the Jesuit order in 1772, the Empress Marie Theresa of Austria assigned the palace to various institutions and today it

The Brera Palace, façade

houses the *Academy of Fine Arts*, the *National Library*, the *Astronomical Observatory* and the *Picture Gallery*.

The Brera Art Gallery
Pinacoteca di Brera

The gallery was conceived in 1776 as the teaching section of the Academy, was promoted to the status of National Gallery during the Napoleonic period and on the 15th of August 1809 was opened with the intention of stimulating a wider public interest in the arts. From an initial modest collection which existed at first, it has become one of the most important galleries in Italy. The collection is composed of donations and acquisitions and, for the most part, of works confiscated by the state between the end of the 18th century and the beginning of the 19th century following the suppression of various religious orders. Today, the thirty-eight rooms contain examples of all the Italian schools, though prevalently those of Lombardy and Venice, as well as a considerable number of foreign works. The picture gallery was badly damaged by bombing during the war, and was completely rebuilt and reorganized in accordance with the latest museum criteria. A project for the complete reorganization and rearrangement of the exhibition spaces has been in progress since 1989.

Room I - Contains the Iesi collection of 20th century paintings and sculpture, including *The Silver Dollar Club* by Afro Basaldella, *Riot in the Galleria* and the *Rising City* by Umberto Boccioni, *Women with a Guitar* by Massimo Campigli, *Rhythms of Objects, Metaphysical Muse, The Enchanted Room, Mother and Son, The House of Love* by Carlo Carrà, *The Sacred Fish, Marine Still-life with Prawns, Marine Still-life with a Lapwing, San Moisè, The Peonies, Marine Still-life* by Filippo De Pisis, *The Balance, Rebel Angel with a White Moon* by Osvaldo Licini, *The Slaughtered Ox* by Mario Mafai, several fine sculptures by Marino Marini (*Pomona Reclining, The Miracle, Pomona, Miracle*), terracotta sculptures by Arturo Martini (*The Drinker, Ophelia*), *Portrait of the Artist Moïse Kisling* by Amedeo Modigliani, *Flowers and Still-life* by Giorgio Morandi, *Bull's Head* by Pablo Picasso, *The Carpenter's Bench* and *Concertina* by Ottone Rosai, *Dame à la Voilette* by Medardo Rosso, *Cardinal Vannutelli on his Death Bed* and *Still-life with Sole* by Scipione (Gino Bonichi), Gino Severini, *The North-South* and *Great Still-life with a Pumpkin* by Gino Severini, *The Truck, The Marvel Factory*, and *The Lamp* by Mario Sironi and *Watermelon and Liquors* by Ardengo Soffici.

Room IA - This room contains a reconstruction of the chapel of Mocchirolo (near Lontate sul Seveso) with its magnificent cycle of Lombard frescoes of the 14th century, attributed to the so-called Master of Mocchirolo. The frescoes represent the *Crucifixion; Christ with the Symbols of the Evangelists; Count Porro with his Family Offering the Model of the Chapel to the Madonna; Holy Knight; Resurrected Christ giving His Blessing.*

Room II - This room and the two that follow it are dedicated to Venetian, Lombard. and other Northern

The Brera Art Gallery, Madonna and Child by A. Lorenzetti (Room II)

Italian painters of the 16th century. Works exhibited here include *St. Veranus with Angels and Stories from His Life* by the so-called Pisan Painter (13th century), Ambrogio Lorenzetti's *Madonna and Child; Christ Enthroned Adored by the Angels* by Giovanni da Milano; *Madonna and Child with Saints by* Lorenzo Veneziano.

Room III - Paintings by J. Bellini, N.di Pietro, A. di Bartolo, G.di Bologna (including his *Madonna and Child with Angels*) and others.

Room IV - Paintings by Gentile da Fabriano (*The Valle Romita Polyptych; Crucifixion)*, Stefano da Verona (*Adoration of the Magi*) and others.

Room V - Dedicated mainly to Venetian painters of the 15th and 16th centuries, including Giovanni d'Alemagna

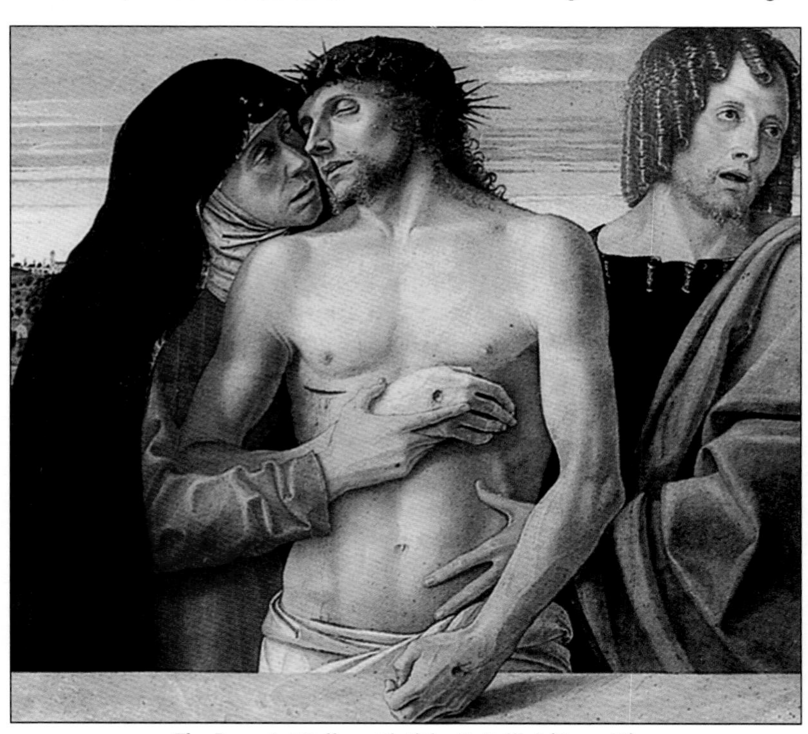

The Brera Art Gallery, Pietà by G. Bellini (Room VI)

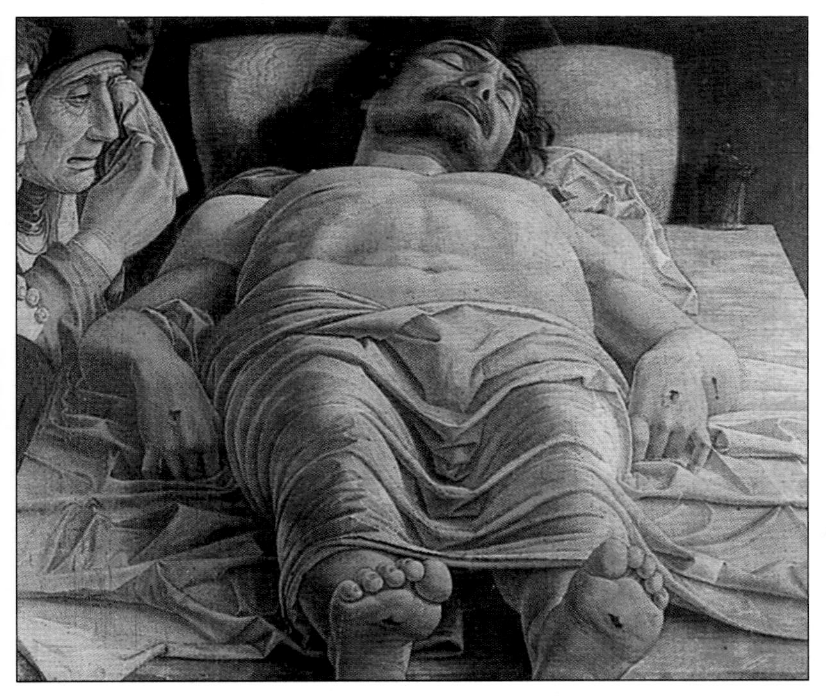

The Brera Art Gallery, Dead Christ in the Sepulcher by A. Mantegna (Room VI)

and Antonio Vivarini (*The Praglia Polyptych*), Pedro Berruguete (*Dead Christ Supported by Two Angels*) Girolamo da Treviso the Elder (*Dead Christ Supported by Two Angels*).

Room VI - Paintings of particular interest in this room include *St. Sebastian* by Liberale da Verona, *St. Stephen disputing with the Doctors of the Sanhedrin* by Vittore Carpaccio, *St. Jerome in the Desert* and *St. Peter on his Throne with St. John the Baptist and St. Paul* by Cima da Conegliano, *Madonna and Child* and *Pietà* by Giovanni Bellini and *The Polyptych of St. Luke* and *Dead Christ in the Sepulcher with Three Mourners* by Andrea Mantegna.

Room VII - This room contains portraits by Venetian artists of the 16th

The Brera Art Gallery, Enthroned Madonna and Child with Saints Andrew, Ursula, Monica and Sigmund, by B. Montagna (Room VII)

The Brera Art Gallery, Madonna of the Rose Garden by B. Luini (Room XIX)

century, including Francesco Torbido called "Il Moro", (*Portrait of a Man*), Titian (*Portrait of Count Antonio Porcia*), Lorenzo Lotto (*Portrait of Laura da Pola, Portrait of Febo da Brescia*), Paris Bordone (*The Venetian Lovers*).

Room VIII - Dedicated mainly to Venetian painters of the 15th century, the most noteworthy of which are Cima da Conegliano (*St. Peter Martyr with St. Nicholas of Bari and St. Benedict, Madonna and Child with Saints and Donors*) Gentile and Giovanni Bellini (*St. Mark Preaching in Alexandria in Egypt*), Palma the Elder (*St. Helen* and *Constantine with Saint Roch and St. Sebastian*), Bartolomeo Montagna (*Enthroned Madonna and Child with St. Francis and St. Bernard, Enthroned Madonna and Child with Saints Andrew, Monica, Ursula, and Sigmund*).

Room IX - In this room paintings by

The Brera Art Gallery, Madonna and Child with Saints by N. Pisano (Room XXII)

Venetian artists of the 16th century are exhibited. The most noteworthy are *St. Jerome in Penitence* by Titian, *Last Supper, Baptism and Temptation of Christ, Christ in the Garden of Gethsemane* by Veronese, *Finding of the Body of St. Mark* and *Pietà* by Tintoretto, *St. Roch Visiting the Plague Victims* by Jacopo Bassano.

Room XIV - Works by 16th century Venetian artists. In particular: Romanino (*Christ with the Cross being carried by a Scoundrel*) Moretto da Brescia (*Madonna and Child*), Giovan Battista Moroni (*Madonna and Child with St. Catherine, St. Francis and Donor*), Gian Gerolamo Savoldo (*Madonna in Glory with the Child, Angels, and Saints Peter, Dominic, Paul and Jerome*), Giovanni Busi called "Il Cariani" (*Enthroned Madonna with Child, Angels and Saints*), Paris Bordone (*Baptism of Christ,*

Holy Family with St. Ambrose and Donor).
Room XV - Lombard paintings and frescoes of the 15th and 16th centuries. Particularly noteworthy are: Gaudenzio Ferrari (*Madonna and Child*), Bramantino (*Madonna and Child with a Man, Crucifix*) Vincenzo Foppa (*Polyptych of the Grazie*), the Master of the Pala Sforzesca (*Sforza altarpiece*), Marco d'Oggiono (*Three Archangels*).
Room XVIII - Lombard paintings of the 16th century. Particularly noteworthy are: *Portrait of Alda Gambara* and *Deposition of Christ* by Altobello Melone, *Venus and Cupid with Two Satyrs* by S. Peterzano, *Self-portrait as the Abbott of the Accademia della Val de Brego* by Giovan Paolo Lomazzo, *Baptism of Christ* by C. Piazza, *Portrait of Lucio Foppa* by G. A.Figino.
Room XIX - 15th and 16th century Lombard religious paintings and portraits, the most distinguished of which are: *Madonna and Child, Saint Catherine of Siena* and a *Cistercian Monk* by Bergognone, *Madonna and Child with St. Joseph and St. Simeon* by Andrea Solario, *Madonna of the Rose Garden* by Bernardo Luini, *Madonna of the Tree* by Cesare da Sesto *and St. John the Baptist* by Donato de' Bardi.
Room XX - 15th century painters from Ferrara and Emilia. Of particular interest are: *St. John the Baptist and St. Peter* by Francesco del Cossa, *Crucifixion* by Cosmè Tura, *Adoration of the Magi* by Lorenzo Costa, *Christ Bearing the Cross* by Francesco Zaganelli.
Room XXI - In this room polyptychs by 15th century artists from the Marches are displayed, including: *St. Peter* by Fra' Cardinale, *The Gualdo Tadino Polyptych* by Girolamo di Giovanni, *Madonna of the Candle, Pietà, Crowning of the Virgin* and *The Camerino Triptych* by Carlo Crivelli.
Room XXII - 15th and 16th century paintings by artists from Ferrara and Emilia. Of particular interest are: *Madonna and Child with Saints* by Marco Palmezzano, *Madonna and Child* by Niccolò Pisano, *Madonna and Child with St. Elizabeth, St. Anne, St. Augustine* and *Blessed Pietro degli Onesti, Resurrection of Lazarus* by Ludovico Mazzolino, *St. Sebastian* by Dosso Dossi, *Deposition* by Garofalo (Benvenuto Tisi) *Crucifixion with the Virgin and Saints* by Ortolano (Giovan Battista Benvenuti).
Room XXIII - 16th century paintings by artists from Ferrara and Emilia. Particularly noteworthy are two paintings by Correggio: *Nativity of Christ with St. Elizabeth and the Young St. John* and *Adoration of the Magi.*
Room XXIV - In this room we can admire important works by Piero della Francesca, Signorelli, Bramante and Raphael. These include the magnificent *Pala Montefeltro* by Piero della Francesca which comes from the Church of S. Bernardino in Urbino and was commissioned by the Duke of Urbino in celebration of the birth of his son Guidobaldo; *Madonna and Child* and *Flagellation of Christ* by Signorelli, Bramante's extraordinary *Christ at the Column* and, of particular interest, Raphael's famous *Marriage of the Virgin* which was painted in 1504 and comes from Città di Castello.
Room XXVII - 15th and 16th century paintings from Central Italy. These include: *Annunciation, St. John the Baptist* and *St. Sebastian* by Timoteo Viti,

The Brera Art Gallery, Nativity of Christ with St. Elizabeth and the Young St. John by Correggio (Room XXIII)

Dispute over the Immaculate Conception by Girolamo Genga, *Andrea Doria Dressed as Neptune* by Bronzino.
Room XXVIII - 17th century paintings from Central Italy. Of particular interest are: *Martyrdom of St. Vitalis* by Barocci, *Adoration of the Magi, The Canaanite Woman, St. Anthony Abbott Preaching to the Hermits* by L. Carracci, *The Samaritan Woman at the Well* by A. Carracci, *Abraham Repudiates Hagar and Ishmael* by Guercino and *St. Peter and St. Paul* by Guido Reni.
Room XXIX - This room is dedicated to Caravaggio and artists of his school and includes Caravaggio's *Supper at Emmaus, St. Jerome* by Giuseppe Ribera known as Spagnoletto, *The Samaritan Woman at the Well* by Giovan Battista Caracciolo and *The Martyrs Valerian, Tiburtius and Cecily* by Orazio Gentileschi.
Room XXX - Lombard paintings of the 17th century. Of particular interest are: *Martyrdom of the Franciscans at Nagasaki* by Tanzio da Varallo, *Madonna of the Rosary* by Cerano (Giovan Battista Crespi), *Mystic Marriage of St. Catherine* by Giulio Cesare Procaccini, and *Martyrdom of St. Rufina and St. Seconda* by Morazzone, Cerano and Procaccini.
Room XXXI - This room and the following one are dedicated mainly to works by non-Italian artists: *Madonna and Son* and *St. Anthony of Padua* by Anton van Dyck, *The Sacrifice of Isaac* by Jacob Jordaens, *Last Supper* by Rubens, *Still-life with Musical Instruments* and *Still-life in a Kitchen* by Evaristo Baschenis, *Portrait of a Knight of Malta* by Bernardo Strozzi, *Madonna and Child with*

The Brera Art Gallery, Marriage of the Virgin by Raphael (Room XXIV)

Angels by Piero da Cortona.
Room XXXII - This rooms contains works by Jan de Beer *(Adoration of the Magi, Nativity, Rest during the Flight to Egypt)*, the Master of the Female Half-Figures (*St. Catherine*), Herman Rode (*Portrait of a Person Praying)* and El Greco (*St. Francis Meditating*).
Room XXXIII - Works by Anton Van Dyck (*Portrait of a Lady*), Rubens and Jan Brueghel (*The Nymph Syringe and Pan*) and Jan Brueghel (*Village*).

Room XXXIV - This room contains 17th century religious paintings including: *Madonna and Child with Saints* by Pompeo Batoni, *Ecce Homo* by Luca Giordano, *Madonna of Carmel with Saints*, the *Prophet Elijah* and *Souls in Purgatory* by Giambattista Tiepolo, *St. Jerome, Crucifixion with Mary Magdalene and Saints* by Pierre Subleyras, *St. Gaetanus Comforting a Dying Man* by Sebastiano Ricci, and *Crucifixion* by Giuseppe Maria Crespi.

Room XXXV - This room and the next are dedicated to Venetian painters of the 18th century, genre paintings and Italian portrait painting and includes works by: Pietro Longhi (*Family Concert, The Tooth-puller*), Bernardo Bellotto (*View of the Gazzada, View of Villa Melzi at the Gazzada*), Canaletto (*View of the Grand Canal*), Piazzetta's masterpiece *Rebecca and Eleazar at the Well* as well as paintings by Francesco Guardi and Tiepolo.

The Brera Art Gallery, St. Anthony Abbott Preaching to the Hermits by Ludovico Carracci (Room XXVIIII)

Hallway - In the hallway between Rooms XXXV and XXXVI various paintings are displayed including Sir Joshua Reynold's *Lord Donoughmore.*

Room XXXVI - Among the various works displayed in this room are: *Portrait of a Gentleman* by Fra' Galgario, *Docker Seated on a Basket, and Docker with*

The Brera Art Gallery, The Supper at Emmaus, by Caravaggio (Room XXIX)

The Brera Art Gallery, Madonna and Child with Saints by Pietro di Cortona (Room XXXI)

a Basket, Eggs and Poultry by Pitocchetto (Giacomo Ceruti).

Room XXXVII - This room and the next one are dedicated mainly to 19th century Italian artists and include: *Self-Portraits* by Giuliano Traballesi, Martin Knoller, Giuseppe Bossi and Domenico Aspari, as well as paintings by Francesco Hayez (*Portrait of the Borri Stampa Family, The Kiss, Portrait of Teresa Manzoni Stampa Borri, The Last Moments of the Doge Marin Faliero, Portrait of Alessandro Manzoni*), Pierre-Paul Prud'hon (*Portrait of Count Giovanni Battista Sommariva),* Federico Faruffini (*Sordello and Cunizza*), Giovanni Segantini (*Spring Pastures*), Silvestro Lega (*The Arbor*) Giovanni Fattori (*The Red Cart*), Andrea Appiani (*Venus and Cupid, Venus and Adonis Bathing, Adonis Held by Venus and Cupid, Death of Adonis*).

Room XXXVIII - In this room the visitor may admire Giovanni Pellizza da Volpedo's famous *Crowd* and Umberto Boccioni's *Self-Portrait.*

The visitor should continue along Via Brera until Via Pontaccio which, to the right, leads to the nearby Piazza S. Marco.

The Brera Art Gallery, View of the Canal in front of St. Mark's by Canaletto (Room XXXV)

The Brera Art Gallery - The Kiss by F. Hayez (XXXVII)

The Brera Art Gallery - The Red Ox-cart by G. Fattori (Room XXXVII)

Church of San Marco

Tradition says this church was founded in 1254 by the Milanese nobleman Lanfranco Settala, who then became a General of the Augustinian order. In the 14th century it was reconstructed on a grander scale, and in the 15th century the family chapels of the nobility along the right nave were added. In 1690 the inside was completely transformed and decorated in Baroque style, upon a design by Francesco Castelli. The façade, restored in 1873 is in Lombard Gothic style and only the decorated ogival portal architrave with *Christ between the Symbols of the Evangelists and Two Saints*, remains of the older construction. In the niches of the tabernacle above it are three small statues of *Saints*. The head of the transept still has the form of the original construction of the 13th century; the Lombard style bell-tower is of the same era.

The **interior** is in the form of a Latin cross with three naves divided by pillars and is completely decorated in Baroque style. The chapels of the right aisle contain some paintings worthy of note; in the first, chapel, frescoes by Lomazzo with *Stories of St. Peter and St. Paul* and altarpiece with *Madonna and Child with Saints*, in the third, on the altar, *St. Mark* by Legnanino. In the fourth, in the cupola, the *Descent of the Holy Ghost* perhaps by Vincenzo Campi. In the fifth, the *Prophets and the Virtues* by Antonio Campi. In the right transept various plaques and sepulchral monuments including, in the middle of the central wall, the *Sarcophagus of Lanfranco Settala* (d. 1264) a work attributed to Giovanni di Balduccio and assistants (14th century). On the right wall are fragments of frescoes of the 14th century. In the chapel, to the left, the *Tomb* with panels in relief, is a work attributed to Giovanni di Balduccio or Matteo da Campione, while the two splendid *Angels* which flank the tomb on the wall opposite are by Giovanni di Balduccio.

The great canvas with the *Nativity of St. Francis* is by Legnanino. In the presbytery on the wall to the right of the great altar, is a canvas with the *Dispute between St. Ambrose and St. Augustine* by Camillo Procaccini; on the left wall *Baptism of St. Augustine*, a fine painting by Cerano (1618). In the left transept to the right: the **Chapel of the Pietà** with a copy of the *Deposition* by Caravaggio above the altar (the original is in the Vatican Museum). In the sacristy, magnificent inlaid wardrobes of the 16th century and an altarpiece with the *Holy Family and St. Sirus* by Bernardino Campi (1569). Along the left nave, on the walls: paintings by various artists, including Legnanino, Camillo Procaccini, Palma the Younger and A. Campi.

From Piazza San Marco, via Fatebenefratelli leads to piazza Cavour where beyond the square, behind the *Monument to Cavour*, via Palestro begins, with the Public Gardens on the left. On the right, at No. 16 is the *Royal Villa* (Villa Reale).

Church of San Marco

Royal Villa
Villa Reale

This mansion was built by Leopold Pollack in 1790 and is one of the most beautiful Neoclassical buildings in Lombardy. The external façade is rectangular with the central part faced with rough-hewn blocks of stone on the ground floor, while the two upper floors are in the Ionic style. The internal façade facing the garden is, however, even more beautiful: it is composed of five sections of which three are protruding and decorated with reliefs of mythological subjects and surrounded on the top floor by a series of statues of divinities. The bas-reliefs on the side tympanums represent the *Chariot of Day* and the *Chariot of Night.* The villa was originally the residence of Prince Lodovico Barbiano di Belgioioso. In 1802, the Cisalpine Republic purchased it in order to present it to Napoleon when he accepted the Presidency of the Republic, and he lived here with his wife Josephine. Eugene Beauharnais, the viceroy of Italy, lived here and in 1857, General Radetzky, until his death, on the 5th of January, 1858. Finally, in 1859, the Villa passed to the Crown of Italy, and then became property of the City Council. In the attractive English style gardens there are sculptures and a small lake with a fountain by Adolfo Wildt. The mansion now houses the Gallery of Modern Art.

Gallery of Modern Art
Galleria d'Arte Moderna

The Gallery contains one of the most complete collections of its kind in Italy and follows the development of 19th century art from Milanese Neoclassicism to the Italian Romantic movement as well as the

The Royal Villa

Gallery of Modern Art, The Washerwomen by Mosè Bianchi

various Italian schools of Realism including the Tuscan Macchiaioli, the Piedmontese, Lombard and Posilippo schools, and shows the influence of French Impressionism on Italian art. Recent acquisitions include the *Marini Museum* and the *Boschi*, the *Fontana*, the *Melotti* and the *Vismara Collections.*

The **Giuseppe Vismara Collection** on the ground floor has works by Modigliani, Picasso, Tosi, Sironi, Morandi and other contemporary Italian and French painters.

The first floor contains the **Marino Marini Museum** with sculptures, drawings and graphic works by this artist as well as a series of portraits of cultural and artistic personalities of the 20th century.

Next comes The **Grassi Collection**, donated to the city of Milan by Nedda Grassi in memory of her son Gino. It is arranged in 13 rooms and includes paintings, designs, textiles, Eastern carpets and Eastern works of art. The 135 paintings constitute the essential part of the collection and the greater part belong to the 19th - 20th centuries. Because of its essentially modern nature the collection has been placed in this gallery. Works by 19th century Italian painters, include S. Lega (*The Haymaker, The Passing of the Holy Sacrament*), T. Signorini (*Clouds at Sunset; Oxen at Pietramala*), G. Fattori (*Great Maneuvers; Trooper; Black Horse*), G. Segantini (*Dead Chamois; In the Stable; Still Life*), G. de Nittis (*Femme aux pompons; Lunch at Posillipo*), A. Mancini *(In Tears; Nude; In the Country*), G. Boldini (*Young American Lady*), D. Ranzoni, il Piccio (*Holy Family*), O. Borrani (*Woman with Candle*). The following 20th century artists are represented: G. Balla (*Child Running; Villa Borghese; Racing Car*), U. Boccioni (*Portrait of the Artist's Mother; Portrait of Signora Casabianca*), G. Morandi (*Landscape; Still Life*), O. Rosai (*Landscape*), Tosi, Spadini, V. Guidi, F. Pirandello, F. Casorati. Works by French

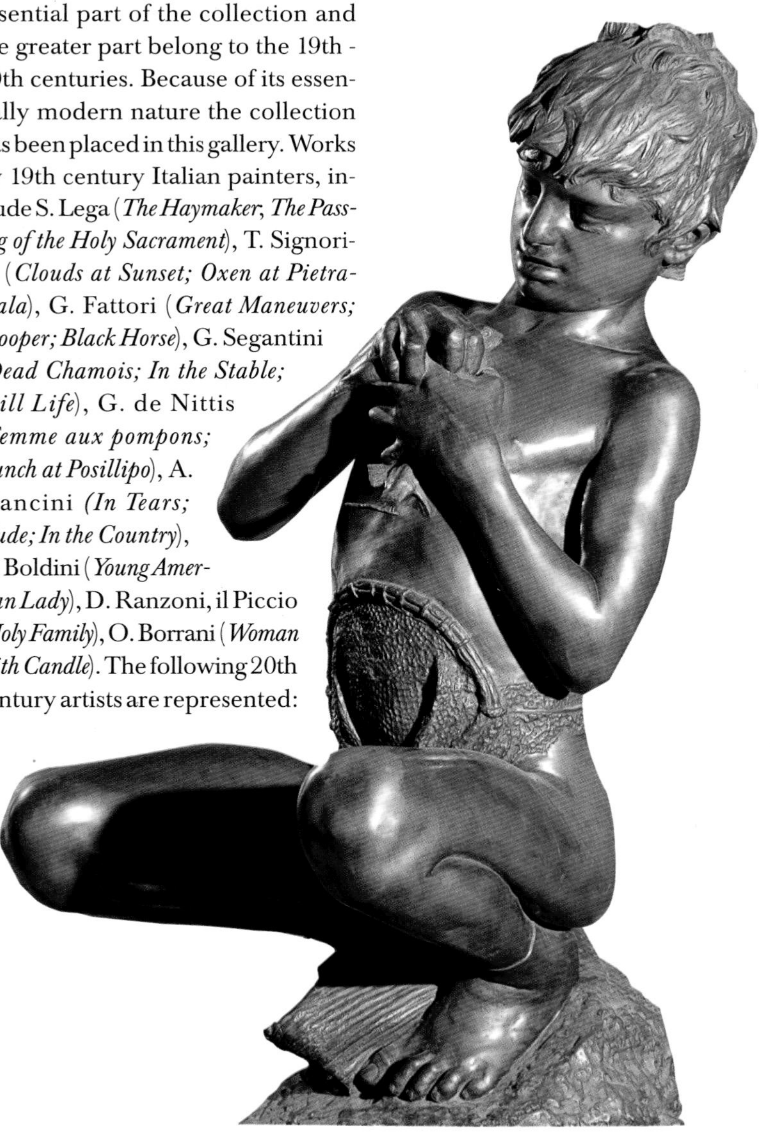

Gallery of Modern Art, The Fisherboy by G. Gemito

Gallery of Modern Art, The Dynamics of the Human Body, by U. Boccioni

painters of the 19th and 20th centuries include: J. B. Corot (*Coup de Vent*; *Lady with a Yellow Flower*), J. F. Millet (*Return to the Farm*), E. Boudin (*Washerwomen*), E. *Manet (Monsieur Armand on Horseback*), P. Cézanne (*Les Voleurs et l'âne*), B. Morisot (*Woman with Flowers*), A. Renoir (*Walk by the Seaside*), P. Gauguin (*Breton Landscape*), E. Vuillard (*Portrait of Mrs. Hessel*), P. Bonnard (*Inside by Lamp Light*), A. Sisley (*Wind and Sun*).

Following the 20th century collection, it used to be possible to visit the Pavilion of Contemporary Art which included paintings and sculpture of the Futurist period and the most recent works of art. On July 27th, 1993 the building was almost entirely destroyed by a terrorist bomb attack which killed five people, a tragic link in the chain of explosions which took place simultaneously in Rome at the churches of Saint John in Lat-

Public Gardens, Monument to Antonio Stoppani by F. Confalonieri

eran and San Giorgio al Velabro. Almost in front of the Royal Villa is the entrance to the **Giardini Pubblici** (public gardens), designed in 1786 by Piermarini and transformed into an English style garden in 1862 by Giuseppe Balzaretto. Within the boundaries of the garden (which extends over an area of 17 hectares) in addition to the Zoo, there are the buildings which house the *Civic Museum of Natural History* which contains several important collections (in particular the ornithological collection with 25,000 specimens), a new set of dioramas and a *planetarium.*

Fourth Itinerary

1 Church of San Maurizio or Great Monastery
2 Basilica of Saint Ambrose
3 Museum of the Basilica of St. Ambrose
4 The Postern of Saint Ambrose
5 The National Museum of Science and Technology
6 Church of Santa Maria delle Grazie
7 Leonardo's Last Supper (Church of Santa Maria delle Grazie)
8 Ambrosian Picture Gallery

On the southern side of Piazza del Duomo, to the left of Palazzo dell'Orologio, lies via degli Orefici which leads into Piazza Cordusio. On the opposite side of the square we take via Dante and immediately to the left is via Meravigli. This in turn leads into Corso Magenta where to the left we find the Church of the Monastero Maggiore (the Great Monastery).

Church of San Maurizio, façade

The Church of San Maurizio or Great Monastery
La chiesa di San Maurizio o Monastero Maggiore

The monastery was built in 1503 by Gian Giacomo Dolcebuono and is of particular interest on account of the quantity of important paintings it contains by the finest artists of the times: Bernardino Luini, who worked there in the first half of the 16th century, as well as Boltraffio and Peterzano.

The interior is very simple with a

Church of San Maurizio, inside

Church of San Maurizio, Scenes of the Martyrdom of St. Catherine of Alexandria (detail) by B. Luini

single nave divided crossways by a wall into two chambers; the first reserved for the congregation; the second for the choir of the nuns. Along the walls are two superimposed orders of pillars, supporting the vault of the ceiling. A series of chapels runs along the lower level, and three-mullioned loggias with graceful little columns adorn the upper level. The walls of the entire church are covered with frescoes. On the internal façade are frescoes by Simone Peterzano with *The Return of the Prodigal Son* and *The Merchants Driven out of the Temple.* The third chapel on the right wall is completely frescoed by Bernardino Luini (his last work-1530*), Scenes of the Martyrdom of St. Catherine of Alexandria.* The frescoes on the wall of the partition are all by Luini, and the *Epiphany* on the altar is by Antonio Campi (1579). The left wall and the chapels are decorated by painters of the 16th century, including several followers of Luini. From the third chapel on the left one enters the **Nun's Choir** which has basically the same structure as the church. Here also the partition wall, which supports the pulpit, is decorated with frescoes by Luini. The scenes which represent the *Road to Calvary* and the *Deposition* are particularly interesting. The upper loggias contain twenty-six roundels frescoed with figures of *Saints* by Boltraffio (1510). On the right of the church is the entrance to the ancient cloister of the Monastery which now houses the **Civic Archeological and Numismatic Collections**. The Museum was inaugurated in 1965 and contains objects which were formerly at Brera and in the Castello Sforzesco and recently excavated archaeological finds.

Continuing along Corso Magenta,

Palazzo Litta

the visitor can admire **Palazzo Litta** on the right, an immense mansion commissioned by count Bartolomeo Arese and built by Francesco M. Richini (1648). The great Rococo façade is by Bartolomeo Bella (1752-63). The portal is flanked by two statues of *Atlas* supporting the balcony. On the upper part of the façade is the coat of arms of the Litta-Visconti-Arese families supported by two *Moors*. In front of Palazzo Litta we find Via Santa Agnese which leads to Piazza Sant'Ambrogio, and, beyond the basilica for which the square is named, is the **Temple of Victory** erected in 1930. This austere and grandiose work is dedicated to the Milanese who lost their lives in the First World War. In the portico, in the niche in front of the entrance, is the great bronze statue of *St. Ambrose*, by Adolfo Wildt.

Temple of Victory

Basilica of Saint Ambrose
Basilica di Sant'Ambrogio

This is one of the oldest churches in Milan and historically one of the most interesting medieval buildings in Lombardy. It was begun in 379, and originally was a small three-nave church with no transept. In 386 it was consecrated by St. Ambrose who, when he died in 397, was buried beside the bodies of St. Gervase and St. Protase inside the Church. In 789 the monastery of the Benedictine Monks was built next to the church and in the 9th century the simple bell-tower, known as the *Monk's Campanile* was added on the right side. The apse and the presbytery were constructed in the 10th century, and then in the 13th century, the aisles, the drum, the atrium and the left bell-tower, known as the *Canon's Campanile* were added. This handsome bell-tower is in Lombard Romanesque style with pilaster strips and friezes of little pendentive arches. It was finished in 1889 with the completion of the three-mullioned loggia. At the end of the 15th century, Cardinal Ascanio Sforza assigned the task of building the cloisters and the portico of the rectory to Bramante. In the following centuries other changes were made, but in 1857 the Archduke Maximilian of Austria ordered that the Baroque additions to the church be removed. It was damaged in the August 1943 bombings, and restored by the architect Ferdinando Reggiori.

The atrium in the form of a rectangular portico, was built in the first half of the 12th century and replaced the orig-

Basilica of Saint Ambrose, aerial view

inal one in front of the church that had been built by the Archbishop Ansperto who governed the Milanese clergy from 868 to 881. The capitals of the pillars in the sturdy portico are adorned with sculptures of plants, symbolic animals and monstrous figures. On the walls of the portico are plaques from tombs, bas-reliefs and the *sarcophagus of Archbishop Ansperto.* The façade, flanked on either side by the two bell-towers, is composed of two loggias, one on top of the other. The top one has a central arch flanked by five arches which diminish in size as they descend; below is the narthex or atrium with its three portals. The great architraves of the two side portals are decorated with carvings inspired by medieval bestiaries. On the sides of the central portal are slender columns supporting an architrave. The original wooden door frames were carved with *Scenes from the Life of David and Saul* made in the 4th or 5th century but completely redone in the 18th century; fragments of the originals are kept in the Mu-

Basilica of Saint Ambrose, façade, atrium and bell-towers

seum of the Basilica. The two panels of the bronze door were made in the 11th - 12th centuries. To the left of the portal, we find the marble *Sepulcher of the Humanist, Pier Candido Decembrio,* (d. 1477) by Tommaso Cazzaniga.

Interior - This majestic and solemn interior has three aisles each terminating with an apse and separated by pillars, with great cross vaults and a *matroneo* or women's gallery along the side aisles. In the central nave the capitals of the pillars are of particular artistic interest; to the right, statue of *Pius IX*, by Francesco Confalonieri (1880). At the third pillar to the left, three frescoes of the 13th century, representing *St. Ambrose, the Madonna and Child* and the donor *Bonamico Taverna.* Further ahead, a column with a *Serpent* in bronze upon it, which according to legend had magical powers; it is a Byzantine work of the 10th century. Near the fifth pillar on the left is the handsome *Pulpit* which was damaged in 1196 when the vaults collapsed and was restored in 1201; it is supported by an ancient sarcophagus which is held aloft by a series of little columns with ornately decorated arches. On the left aisle side: an 11th century bas-relief with the *Last Supper* and also, of the same era, the *Angel and Eagle* in copper which decorate the front of the lectern. Under the pulpit is an *Early Christian Sarcophagus* of the 4th century which, according to tradition contains the remains of Stilicho, the general of Theodoric, and his wife Serena. The sides of the sarcophagus are decorated with reliefs: *Jesus with the Apostles* on the front, *Elijah on the Chariot* and *Baby Jesus between*

Basilica of Saint Ambrose, inside

Basilica of Saint Ambrose, frontal of the Golden Altar

the Ox and the Ass on the right, another relief of *Jesus with the Apostles* in the rear; the *Sacrifice of Abraham* and *Apostles* on the left. At the center of the presbytery rises the **Ciborium**, surmounted by a lofty drum supported by four porphyry columns with capitals, made in the 9th century.

The colored stucco decoration on the baldachin (a canopy structure in masonry) is 13th century and depicts *Christ Offering the Keys to St. Peter and the Book of Wisdom to St. Paul*, on the front; *St. Ambrose between Two Praying Figures* to the right; *St. Ambrose between Saint Gervase and Saint Protase*, on the side facing the apse; *Female Saint between Two Praying Figures*, to the left. Beneath the ciborium we find the famous **Golden Altar** of 835, by the master goldsmith Volvinius, donated by the Archbishop Angilberto II (824-59). The frontal panels show *Redeemer between the Symbols of the Evangelists and the Apostles* and around it *Stories from the Life of Jesus*; on the back, *Stories from the Life of St. Ambrose*; on the sides, *Angels and Saints.* At the sides of the ciborium are two cupboards and the *Abbot's Throne.* The apse, which is built over the crypt, has the

Basilica of Saint Ambrose, detail of the ciborium

remains of the beautiful two-row choir stalls of the 15th century around it, with inlaid *Scenes from the Life of St. Ambrose*; in the center, a marble *Bishop's Throne* of the 9th century. The apse (which was reconstructed after being damaged during the last war) contains Byzantine style mosaics of various epochs in the dome which depict *Christ Giving His Benediction between St. Gervase and St. Protase* in the center and, on the sides, two episodes of the vision of *St. Ambrose at the Funeral of St. Martin of Tours.* From the sides of the presbytery one enters the **Crypt**, divided into two rooms; the first, which dates back to the 9th and 11th centuries, was renovated in 1740 and has five aisles supported by red marble columns: the second, surrounded by railings, holds the *Urn of the Patron Saints* with the remains of St. Ambrose, St. Gervase and St. Protase, by Giovanni Lomazzi from designs by Ippolito Marchetti (1897), in glass and silver. Behind, is the porphyry tomb where the bodies of the three Saints were found in 1864 along with a column from Piazza Castello which indicated the place of the martyrdom of St. Gervase and St. Protase. Along the right aisle are seven chapels. On the altar of the second chapel is the *Madonna, St. Bartholomew* and the *Baptist*, altarpiece attributed to Gaudenzio Ferrari. In the fifth chapel, which is Baroque in style, are two great 18th century canvases with the *Deaths of St. Benedict and St. Bernard* and below, two fragments of frescoes in the style of Luini with *Jesus in the Garden* and the *Entry of Jesus into Jerusalem.* In the sixth chapel there are some remarkable works by Lanino with the *Madonna and Child and St. John* on the altar and *Stories of St. George* on the walls. The seventh chapel is closed at the end by the altar with *St. Ambrose in Agony*, an altarpiece by Andrea Lanzani (17th century); to the left one enters the ante-chapel of Saint Satirus with frescoed vaults by Antonio de Giorgi representing the *Glory of St. Victor* (1763).

Basilica of Saint Ambrose, tombstone inside the church

One now comes to the 4th century **Sepulchral Chamber of St. Vic-**

tor in the Golden Sky (San Vittore in Ciel d'Oro), which contained the remains of St. Victor and St. Satirus. It is a square chamber with an apse covered by a dome decorated with gleaming golden mosaics of the 5th century, showing *a bust of St. Victor.* On the walls are other mosaics of the same epoch representing, to the left *St. Ambrose between St. Gervase and St. Protase,* and, to the right *St. Felix, St. Materno* and *St. Naborre.* In the crypt below, a 5th century sarcophagus, which was later used as a place to put relics of the martyrs. To the left of the Sepulchral Chamber, one enters the **Sacristy of the Masses**, the vault of which was painted by Tiepolo with the *Glory of Saint Bernard,* but the fresco was destroyed by the 1943 bombings. Two detached frescoes by Tiepolo have now been put in its place; they are the *Martyrdom of Saint Victor* and the *Shipwreck of Saint Satirus* (1737). Going back once more into the church, to the first span of the left aisle, we find the *Cherubs Picking Grapes* of the 5th- 6th centuries on the architrave of a door. Continuing along the aisle, in the first chapel, beyond the baptismal font, we find the fresco of *Christ Risen between Two Angels,* by Bergognone (1491); the frescoed *Paradise* is by Isidoro Bianchi (17th century); a roundel with *Madonna* by Luini on the altar of the third chapel. Through a door at the end of the aisle, the **Portico of the Rectory**, which was begun in 1492 by Bramante for Ludovico il Moro. It was intended to be a four-sided cloister, but in 1499 building was suspended when Ludovico fell from power, so only the side next to the basilica was finished. The great archways are supported by columns, four of which are made to look like tree trunks. Half way along the portico on the wall behind the arch, are two reliefs with the busts of *Ludovico il Moro* and *Beatrice d'Este,* end of the 15th century. In the courtyard of the rectory is the **Oratory of St. Sigmund**, which was originally called Santa Maria Greca. It has been modified many times since the 11th century and was finally restored in 1940. It is preceded by a portico with arches and columns from ancient Roman buildings. Remains of the 15th century decorations are still preserved on the inside.

Museum of the Basilica of Saint Ambrose

The entrance to the Museum is at the end of the Rectory portico. The museum was founded in 1949, and includes numerous relics and artifacts related to the long and glorious history of the Basilica. The **Treasure** is placed half way down the flight of stairs. One of the most extraordinary examples of the goldsmith's art, is the *Processional Cross,* of the 15th century. On the landing, a medallion in stucco with the *Bust of St. Ambrose* of the 12th century is placed between the two doors; from this point one enters Room I

known as the *Tapestry Room.* In Room II, the *Textile Room*, there are precious textiles, known as the *Dalmatics of St. Ambrose* which include a 4th century damask of Eastern origin with hunting scenes. There are also pieces of fabrics from the sarcophagus of the Saint found in 1940 in the Cappella del Transito. In Room III, *Room of the Altar Frontals*, we can admire the triptych by Bernardino Zenale representing the *Madonna with St. Ambrose and St. Jerome* (1494). There are also various altar frontals including an embroidered one of the 15th century. Pieces of the bombs which hit the basilica in 1943 are displayed in the corridor. Room IV is known as the *Bedstead Room* because an ancient bedstead is displayed in the center of the room which, it is believed, belonged to St. Ambrose and upon which, it seems, the Saint died. Also noteworthy is the reproduction of the ancient doors of the basilica which include several fragments of wood from the original 4th century ones in an exquisite Classical style. Room V, known as the *Fresco Room*, houses interesting works which include *Jesus among the Doctors*, a fresco by Bergognone, and the *Madonna of the Milk*, by Luini. The showcases contain some of the 55 parchment codices which demonstrate the superb quality of Lombard manuscript illumination from the 10th to the 13th centuries. Room VI, the *Historical Room,* contains tapestries of the 16th century, drawings, prints and documents.

The Postern of Saint Ambrose
Pusterla di S. Ambrogio

After leaving the basilica of St. Ambrose, on the right hand side of Via S. Vittore, we find the Postern of St. Ambrose, which is a little door with a double barrel-vault flanked by two towers. It was originally a city-gate, opened in 1171 in the old circle of the medieval walls, and restored in 1940. On the façade, facing towards Via De Amicis above the double barrel-vault, is a tabernacle with Gothic statues representing *St. Ambrose, St. Gervase* and *St. Protase.*

Along Via S. Vittore there is a small square on the left with the **Basilica of San Vittore al Corpo**, known also as the *Basilica Porziana.* It is of Early Christian origin but was reconstructed by Vincenzo Seregni in 1560. The inside, which is ornately decorated with frescoes and stucco-work, contains remarkable works of art by artists

Postern of Saint Ambrose

Basilica of San Vittore al Corpo

of the 17th century, including Procaccini, Del Cairo, Enea Salmeggia known as "il Talpino", Nuvolone and Daniele Crespi. On the left of the basilica is the *Monastery of St. Victor* which contains the *Leonardo da Vinci National Museum of Science and Technology.*

The Leonardo da Vinci National Museum of Science and Technology

The Museum, which was inaugurated on February 15th, 1953 and named after Leonardo, occupies the ancient Monastery of the Olivetans, near the Basilica of San Vittore. It was completely rebuilt after the damage done to it during the last war and restored to its former solemn and elegant appearance. The purpose of the Museum is to illustrate, in the most attractive way possible, the history of science and technology in action, and the phenomena which led to great inventions, discoveries, and the machines which have contributed so much to technical progress in the modern world. But in contrast with similar institutions in other countries, the Milan museum is arranged according to the three main themes of

Convent of the Olivetans

National Museum of Science and Technology, the Leonardo da Vinci gallery

Leonardo's Humanism: Science, Technology and Art, so the visitor can see ancient and modern machines side by side with experiments in physics taking place, old and new instruments in the glass cases, along with famous paintings, decorations, rooms and reconstructions of environments, all of which help to make an unusually varied and fascinating exhibition.

The imposing *Leonardo Gallery*, is dominated by the austere *self-portrait* of the great Master himself, etched on to a sheet of crystal glass. The Gallery contains the richest, most faithfully reconstructed collection in the world of models of machines, devices and projects by Leonardo. In addition, the Museum has a historical *Gallery of Physics* with a teaching section, which holds the apparatus and instruments (originals and copies) used by Galileo, Newton, Volta, Pacinotti, Ferraris, and others, and active participation showcases where it is possible to perform experiments which illustrate phenomena, laws and principles of physics. The *Optics Room* in particular is set up in order to illustrate the fundamental principles of geometric optics (reflection, refraction, total reflection, lenses) and polarization (rotating and photoelastic) and spectroscopy (emission spectra, absorption spectra, photographic spectra), Roentgen rays (X-rays), fluorescence, etc. The *Radio*

and Telecommunications Section is in the *Marconi Room* and houses the most important apparatus invented and built by Marconi, including those once mounted aboard the yacht "*Elettra*". Note the "*Pantelegraph*" by G. Caselli (1855), the first device used in public service for the transmission of images along telegraph wires. In the *Typewriter Section* the "*Cembalo scrivano*" (Writing Clavichord) by A. Ravizza (1855). The Museum also possesses a *Naval Section*, a *Clock Section* with many valuable pieces, a collection of antique gold artifacts, a *Transport Section* which includes a great illustrated panel of the evolution of the wheel from the Ur wheel (4000 B.C.) to the modern wheel with tires. Among the exhibits in the basement: a steam engine by Horn (around 1830); the first engines (wind-driven, hydraulic, and thermal); the history of metal casting, of metallurgy and of the working of metals (rolling mills, a water hammer of the 18th century which still works perfectly). Also of interest, the magnificent *Great Hall of the Columns* which once housed the library of the convent, the *Hall of the Last Supper* with its ornate 18th century decorations, and the *Hall of the Cinema*. Other lesser halls frequently house congresses and meetings of great cultural interest and international importance. The *Museum Library* contains books on the history of science. The *Teaching Center for Experimental Physics*, with its classrooms and collection of instruments, and the *Scientific and Technological Journal Room* are additional facilities which integrate the activity of the various sections and provide a valuable source of information and research assistance for visitors and scholars.

Continuing along Via S. Vittore, we take a right turn along Via Bernardino Zenale which leads once more to Corso Magenta. Immediately ahead lies Piazza Santa Maria delle Grazie, with the church of the same name.

National Museum of Science And Technology, two rooms with transportation exhibits

Church of Santa Maria delle Grazie

Of all the churches in Milan, Santa Maria delle Grazie is one of the most inspiring. It is a blend of Gothic and Renaissance styles created by Guiniforte Solari and Donato Bramante and was built on the site where a chapel with a fresco of the *Madonna*, known as *Madonna delle Grazie*, once stood. The construction of the church, which was designed by Guiniforte Solari and com-

Church of Santa Maria delle Grazie

missioned by the Dominican Order, was started in 1466, when the adjoining Monastery was practically finished, and completed in 1490. Shortly afterwards, however, Ludovico il Moro, who was very fond of this church, decided to modify and enlarge it with the intention of creating a memorial to himself and his wife, Beatrice d'Este. After the original presbytery and apse were demolished, Bramante began constructing the magnificent tribune which consisted of a great cube with three apses and a marvelous decoration of roundels along the bands of the base, with Sforza coats of arms and medallions in marble, and men and women *Saints* attributed to Amadeo in the upper portions. Within the tribune rises the polygonal drum with mullioned windows and a graceful gallery supporting the dome. In 1497 Beatrice d'Este was buried in this church but, on account of the tumultuous political situation at the time he died, Ludovico il Moro could not be buried beside her and the statues by Solari for their tombs are now in the Charterhouse of Pavia. From 1558 to 1782 the *Tribunal of the Inquisition* had its headquarters in the monastery. In 1934-37 the whole building was consolidated and restored under the direction of the architect Piero

Church of Santa Maria delle Grazie, the apse

Portaluppi, thanks to the generosity of the senator Ettore Conti, who then also financed the 1947 renovations made necessary after the serious damage done to the Refectory of the Monastery and the main body of the Church during the 1943 bombings. The low, wide façade is in traditional Lombard style. It is divided vertically by pilaster strips and has four Gothic windows in the lower part and round windows (oculi) in the upper part. The marble porch in the form of a shrine, which is supported by two columns and pillars, is by Bramante. In the lunette of the arch overhead is a fresco by Michelangelo Bellotti (1729). Along the right side of the church are pairs of ogival windows with round oculi set between the points of each pair.

Interior - The church has three naves divided by wide ogival arches supported by columns and with cross vaults with various frescoed decorations. Along the side aisles runs a series of square chapels. Above the arches of the nave, in the lunettes, there are roundels with half figures of *Dominican Saints* by Bernardino Butinone and full figures of *Dominican Saints* on the pillars (15th century) also by Butinone. In the first chapel of the right aisle, on the left wall, the *Tombs of the Della Torre family*, with three bas-reliefs on the front of the sarcophagus showing the *Annunciation*, the *Adoration of the Shepherds* and the *Epiphany*, by Francesco Cazzaniga (1483). Above the altar is a beautiful fresco removed from its original site, the *Madonna adoring the Child*, by an unknown Lombard artist of the 15th century. Second chapel: four 16th century cenotaphs (empty tombs which serve as burial monuments). The fourth chapel is decorated with frescoes by Gaudenzio Ferrari (1542) with *Stories of the Passion* and *Angels*. In the fifth chapel the walls are decorated with stucco *Angels Bearing Festoons* (16th century). The chapel vault and the upper sections of the walls are decorated with frescoes by Giovanni De'Mio. The sixth chapel has a *Madonna and Saints*, by Coriolano Malagnazzo (16th century) on the altar and frescoes on the walls by the Fiammenghini brothers. The seventh chapel frescoes

Church of Santa Maria delle Grazie, inside

Church of Santa Maria delle Grazie, cloister

and stucco-work on the vault are by Ottavio Semini and *The Baptist Worshipped by Count Vimercati*, by Marco d'Oggiono. We now come to the apse by Bramante with its four great arches holding the dome which is supported by a drum surrounded by a loggia crowned by a decorative frieze: the entire structure is considered a perfect example of Renaissance art. The presbytery is square in form and opens into a great niche. The vault is umbrella shaped, with round oculi in the lunettes at its base. On the walls are incised figures of *Dominican Saints*. In the pendentives of the arches and of the lunettes, are medallions with busts of the *Evangelists* and the *Doctors* attributed to Amadeo. The beautiful wooden choir has two rows of inlaid stalls with figures of *Saints* and floral motifs (1470-1510). Between the presbytery and the left nave is the **Chapel of the Madonna delle Grazie** which was the oratory of the first church built here, which was then incorporated into the subsequent structure and later enlarged and decorated with stuccos and paintings, unfortunately mostly destroyed by the 1943 bombings. On the front of the span facing the nave is a great 17th century composition in stucco showing the *Madonna, Angels and Saints* on a blue background; the 17th century painting over the entrance arch is by Cerano. On the altar is the *Madonna delle Grazie*, a much venerated image during the plagues of 1576 and 1630. The fourth chapel of the left aisle (Chapel of Senator Conti), closed off by a 17th century bronze railing, has a triptych on the altar with the *Madonna and Saints* by Niccolò da Cremona. In the second chapel, are the *Funeral Stelae of Cardinal Arcimboldi* with sculptures attributed to Bambaia and the *Funeral plaques of Cardinal Branda Castiglioni* (d. 1495). In the first chapel, the remains of frescoes by Montorfano, and a modern bas-relief by Arrigo Minerbi on the altar. Returning to the apse, through a door to the left, we enter the **Small Cloister** by Bramante which Ludovico il Moro commissioned. It is a small court with a harmonious portico on all four sides; the arches are supported by graceful tapered columns with exquisitely worked capitals. In the lunette of the door which leads to the church, on both sides of a small shrine, is a fresco with *St. Peter and St. Catherine*, by Bramantino who also painted the one in the lunette above the portal on the opposite side of the portico with *Madonna and Child with Saints*. The door leads into the **Old Sacristy**, also by Bramante with great wardrobes on two levels all round the walls, inlaid and painted with *Stories from the Old and New Testaments* (1497-1503). On the internal faces of the side pillars of the apse are bas-reliefs with portraits of *Ludovico il Moro* and his son *Maximilian*.

Last Supper by Leonardo Da Vinci

To the right of the church is the ex-monastery of the Dominicans. In the Refectory of the monastery Ludovico il Moro commissioned Leonardo to paint the Last Supper (1495-98), one of the world's greatest masterpieces of art. The painting occupies all of the wall at the end of the refectory; in the three lunettes over the fresco, below the decorations of the vault (which was destroyed in 1943) are the coats of arms of the Sforza and the Este families surrounded by wreaths, a tribute to the Duke Ludovico il Moro and his wife, Beatrice d'Este. Some scholars maintain that the scene by Leonardo of the twelve Apostles seated together with their Lord at the supper table, portrays them at the moment when Jesus announced that one of them would betray him, or, as others say, at the moment of the Consecration. The reaction of the Disciples is apparent from their exaggerated gestures, emotional movements and facial expressions, and contrasts with the immobility of Christ who dominates the scene from the center of a rigorously symmetrical composition in perfect perspective. The whole scene seems to be bathed in a diffused, gentle light coming partly from the three windows at the far end of the room and partly from the light at the front from the actual window in the real room. The painting was miraculously left undamaged by the bombings of August 1943 which partially destroyed the nearby cloisters and parts of the church. Unfortunately the fresco has always had conservation problems. Since 1517 it has steadily deteriorated, mainly because of the new painting technique used by Leonardo as an experiment. At the time of Napoleon the refectory was used as a stable and in 1801 was flooded by water. In 1953 the fresco was cleaned and consolidated; a complex and radical restoration procedure was completed in the second half of the 1990s so that this marvelous work can now be seen by the public again.

Bartholomew — James the Lesser — Andrew — Judas — Peter — John — Jesus Christ — Thomas — James the Greater — Philip — Matthew — Jude (Thaddaeus) — Simon